Hooked Rug
★ for Baby & Beyond ★
Inspiration for a Family Heirloom

by Norma Batastini

Presented by

R.U.G HOOKING

Copyright © 2019 by Ampry Publishing LLC
Published by
AMPRY PUBLISHING LLC
3400 Dundee Road, Suite 220
Northbrook, IL 60062
www.amprycp.com

www.rughookingmagazine.com

Graphic Design by Matt Paulson
On the cover: *Noel, Noel*, designed and hooked by Norma Batastini.

Printed in the United States of America
10 9 8 7 6 5 4 3 2 1

Photography by Impact Xpozures, unless otherwise noted
Cataloging-in-Publication Data
Library of Congress Control Number: 2019935102

978-1-945550-38-6

Table of Contents

Dedication

This book is dedicated to my mother, Ellen Savage, who has been my champion for my entire life. She always encouraged me to follow my dreams and turn my ideas into reality, especially in rug hooking.

The inspiration for this book came from the births of my grandson, Jack McPherson Batastini, and my granddaughter, Addison Grace Batastini.

Acknowledgments

My family has been truly supportive of this book and all that was required to make the included projects. Everyone wanted to help in whatever way they could. My daughter Meredith took over most of the cooking duties while I was working on the final pages. My son Matthew, a lawyer, reviewed the copyright sections so they would be understandable for moms, grandmas, and aunts.

The Heart in Hand Rug Hooking Group jumped right in from the start and offered to hook or finish many of the projects.

Other students I have taught throughout the country were also eager to help with the book by making and designing special projects.

Bill Bishop did most of the photography and really makes everything look so good.

And finally, Sandy Bennington, a friend, rug hooker, and retired English teacher, did all of the final editing as I was battling a serious illness. She made the text sing!

Introduction

"When we treat children's play as seriously as it deserves, we are helping them feel the joy that's to be found in the creative spirit. It's the things we play with and the people who help us play that make a great difference in our lives."
—Fred Rogers

"Play" is a word often used by rug hookers when talking about the pleasures and processes involved in making a rug. Playing with color . . . playing with motifs . . . playing in the dye pot . . . playing with wool . . . These are some of the phrases we use, and what these phrases are really saying is that we are having fun! There are no bounds to our thoughts. We are setting aside rules and our usual way of doing things, and we are embracing new ideas. It's almost as if we are children, spontaneously discovering the fun of letting our imagination and creative spirit lead us.

This is the spirit in which I approached the subject of this book: hooking for children.

I've always enjoyed children—my own, my nieces and nephews—and now my grandchildren. I especially enjoy playing with them! I have collections of dolls, games, stuffed animals, and children's books. Maybe you do, too! Many of these treasures (now considered collectibles) are from my own childhood, and they hold many memories of that time and of the relatives who gave them to me.

Some of these treasures are the toys that my own children played with as they were growing up. They hold many memories, not only of my children, but also of my experiences as a parent.

As you think about the children whom you cherish in your own life, you will find that every stage of their lives offers opportunities for rug hookers to play: a birth, a special interest or adventure, an achievement (such as college graduation). Perhaps as you read this right now, you are beginning to dream about a rug that you can create for one of the children in your life.

I have been inspired to create rugs that grew out of the activities and interests of my children. The first was a rug for my toddler son. I was making a quilt for his bed with the Bear Paw block design. He had picked the colors. At the time I was taking a beginner's rug-hooking class and we were to choose a geometric design. My choice was easy—I designed a rug to coordinate with the quilt. I used the Bear Paw block design and created a border for each end with bears and pine trees. The colors I used were similar to those in the quilt but a bit more muted.

The second rug was for my daughter. I was taking a series of classes with Patsy Becker and chose her pattern *Posey Cat*. My daughter loves all animals, especially cats, so *Posey Cat* was just right for her. I hooked it in the colors that she liked, pinks and soft teals.

I mention both of these rugs because they involved a lot of creative energy for me. I was a relative newbie at rug hooking and was eager to try lots of new things. In *Bear Paw Tracks* I worked out the math involved in a geometric design, but my creative spark was to add the borders. I worked out the colors to match the quilt, but my creative spark was to add multicolored wool to jazz up the color plan.

In *Posey Cat*, I played with the direction of hooking, varying it as is typical in a primitive style. The background was hooked by echoing each motif with a variety of as-is camel-colored wool. At the time this rug was hooked, the camel wools were similar in appearance. After being on my daughter's bedroom floor for many years, the rug has faded overall, and the background wools have faded at different rates. My son's rug was also well used and has the patina of age. The fading just adds to the specialness of each rug as part of my children's lives.

If you are looking for a children's theme for a rug, there are many commercial patterns available. Although the design has already been done, your creative spirit can make it a unique rug that you will love to hook and love to give to a special child in your life.

If you want to create your own design, you can begin by thinking about simple shapes and start to "play" with all the elements that go into a rug.

Regardless of the age of the child who will receive your gift, this book will inspire you! It includes ideas for rugs, small mats, pillows, footstools, and toys. Genres covered include nursery rhymes and songs, storybook tales, sports, animals, games, and much more. Some favorite patterns are included for your use. In addition, there is a resource list for many of the featured items. Please note that some of the rugs pictured in this book are copyrighted by the artist and may not be copied.

As we make our rugs, each of us needs to know about copyright laws. To help you understand the importance of honoring copyright, I've included an overview of commonsense guidelines.

Several chapters of the book begin with a quote from Fred Rogers. His television show was a favorite in our house. He inspired many in his lifetime and the US Postal Service has even issued a stamp in his honor. Fred Rogers was the commencement speaker at my son's college, and all the graduates sang, "It's a Beautiful Day in the Neighborhood" for him. I imagine that most of you can also sing it! It brought tears to many eyes. Maybe someday I'll hook a rug depicting some of his famous cardigans.

When hooking a rug for a child, view it as a time to let your creativity run wild! Play with design ideas, use unfamiliar colors, and hook with a sense of joy. Remember that young children haven't learned the rules and their artwork is pure and simple. Older children in high school and college are experimental in their approach to art, breaking the boundaries. Be open to new ideas and challenge yourself artistically . . . behave like a child!

Bear Paw Tracks, 22" x 38", wool on linen. Designed and hooked by Norma Batastini, Glen Ridge, New Jersey, 1996.

Posey Cat, 30" x 22", wool on monk's cloth. Designed and hooked by Norma Batastini, Glen Ridge, New Jersey, 1996.

Commonsense Thoughts about Copyright Rules for Rug Hookers

Copyright laws are very complex and can be hard to interpret for our rug-hooking projects. To help me understand, I keep in mind a quote from Robert Fulghum: "All I really I need to know, I learned in kindergarten." Keep it simple. If an idea or design is not your own, don't copy it without permission.

You do not want to break copyright law and you do not want your work to become a victim of copying. Every country had its own copyright laws, so it is important to know the laws that apply to you. There is no international copyright law.

I am not a lawyer and am not qualified to give legal advice. My understanding of copyright laws as applicable to rug-hooking projects has evolved from conversations with other rug hookers as well as from my own research. Specific questions about copyright and potential copyright infringement should be referred to lawyers with appropriate expertise in this area. Below are some general guidelines I have adopted for my own work:

- Generally, if something was published before 1923, it is in the public domain and is not protected by copyright law; you may use it. There are many patterns of antique rugs from the late 1800s and early 1900s that can be used.

- Work created after 1923 is copyright protected from the date of the artist's death plus 70 years. Therefore, most contemporary works are protected. For instance, Georgia O'Keefe died in 1986, so her work is protected an additional 70 years, until 2056. In addition, the estates of some famous artists may have extended the original copyright.

- Many copyright-free images are available in print or on the Internet. They are given freely and may be used for individual use. But not every image on the Internet can be freely used; some do have restrictions.

- When possible, use your own drawings or photographs for your designs. For instance, I drew a pattern of the New York skyline. I spent a morning photographing the skyline from two different locations. I referred to those photos when designing the pattern.

- If you need to use reference materials, keep notes of your sources. For instance, when drawing birds, I often look at *Field Guide to Birds*, by Roger Tory Peterson. I don't copy an image; I check on details such as the length of the tail or the shape of the beak.

- If you are determined to use a copyrighted design, get permission. This may be difficult with famous artists and large companies, but most have a contact for media or customer service that may help. Not-yet-famous artists are usually flattered that you have asked and just ask to see the finished work.

- Any original design you create is copyright protected as soon as you make it. If you want to share your work, make sure you clearly explain your terms and restrictions on use. For instance, are you sharing with a friend for one-time use or giving to a patternmaker who will profit from sale of the pattern?

- Fair Use is a doctrine originating in the US and was included in the Copyright Act of 1976. It allows for the use of copyrighted work in special circumstances. These include teaching, research, news reporting, criticism, and commentary. Once a hooked rug is displayed or exhibited as a work of art, it no longer fits this definition, unless you are a teacher using the work in order to critique or comment on it.

- Trademark is a sign, logo, or symbol that is recognizable and represents products or services. An individual or a business can own a trademark. An example is the McDonald's Golden Arches logo. Usually a copyright symbol is prominently displayed on products or labels.

Jack and the Beanstalk, *70" x 27", wool on linen. The design was a free pattern in the magazine* American Home, *copyrighted in 1957. Hooked by Evelyn Lawrence, Hallstead, Pennsylvania, 2018.*

The original pattern, as printed in the magazine, was to be painted on a door. This piece is painted with wool and is intended to hang on the door with each height addition written on the side of the door or woodwork. It could also hang in a hallway.

Pattern provided on page 107

Baby Blocks, *5" cubes. Wool on linen backing, finished with wool batting over foam blocks. Designed by Norma Batastini and hooked by Karen Bellinger, Fair Lawn, New Jersey, and Norma Batastini, Glen Ridge, New Jersey, 2017.*

Chapter 1

Baby Makes Three

The wonderful news arrives: a baby is expected! These joyous words affect all of us, whether we are a parent, grandparent, aunt, uncle, sister, brother, or friend. Everything is now changed. Anticipation and excitement build. There is so much to plan and do! Knitting needles come out. Crochet hooks start moving. Quilts begin to take shape. And, of course rugs are hooked. All of this is being done for the tiny new arrival.

In this chapter I will explore ideas for the baby's room. (Remember that the things you make for this early stage of the baby's life will be part of the décor, not things to be played with or used!) You will be facing three challenges:

The first challenge is to make something that fits in with the chosen color scheme of the nursery. What colors will the prospective parents want or use? Remember that the colors and motifs they choose may not be the ones that you would choose! Today's young parents are registering at stores like Pottery Barn Kids, Buy Buy Baby, Target, and Crate and Barrel, so you can see their preferences in these stores or online. When you hook something in the parents' chosen colors, you will help to ensure that whatever you have hooked will be used and loved instead of relegated to the back of a closet! If their color choices are not your favorites, consider your work as an artistic exercise.

The biggest surprise for me when I was first checking out the merchandise available for babies was the ubiquitous use of gray. Gray is not a color that I often use in rug hooking, and planning around it was hard. (See the sidebar on page 11 about using gray.)

The second challenge you face is to choose an appropriate design. You may fall in love with the motifs on the parent's selection of bedding for the baby's crib, but remember that motifs on store items are usually copyrighted. Graphic artists and fabric designers spend many hours creating appealing designs. It is tempting to copy these delightful images—but don't. They are protected by copyright and belong to the company that produces them.

Here is an example from my own experience: My granddaughter, Addison, has a room decorated in gray, white, and yellow, with elephant motifs from a Pottery Barn Kids collection. Although elephant images in general cannot be copyrighted, that specific elephant shape, as well as the arrangement of that shape on the bedding and other items in the Pottery Barn Kids design, are copyright protected. Likewise, the colors alone cannot be copyrighted but if they are arranged in specific patterns, those patterns could be copyrighted.

Here is where you can exercise creativity! I chose to hook a gray elephant-shaped pillow and another pillow in a geometric design that included elephants. I was able to use the main motif and the colors of the nursery décor successfully without breaking copyright laws. With the geometric pillow I added pink and green into the color palette (with approval from my son and daughter-in-law).

The third challenge is to make items that will be cherished for generations. A baby grows so quickly; will a piece that is so charming and cute for an infant be soon outgrown? Hooking takes time, and we want these lovely hooked pieces to last. Consider how items could continue to be used in a toddler's room or a teenager's room—maybe even in a college dorm!

This is why I think pillows are always a good option. They can be made into many different shapes and may be used on a bed, a chair, or the floor. In the baby's nursery, a pillow can be used with a rocker when the baby is being fed. In the toddler's room, a pillow can be used while the child is playing on the floor, or on the bed while reading, to prop up storybooks. For the teenager, pillows can be used anywhere as they read, do homework, or hang out with friends.

Be sure to use a good quality polyester-filled pillow form to fit the shape of your hooked piece. (Just as you always choose good-quality wool to hook with.) If planning an unusual size for the pillow, shop for the pillow form first to check for availability. You can also make your own custom-size form using cotton muslin and a bag of polyester stuffing. Finish the pillow so that the stuffing can be taken out if it someday needs to be cleaned; spills do happen. For the closure, use a zipper, snaps, fabric ties, or Velcro. Buttons may be a swallowing hazard, so you will not want to use them for items for children under three years old.

No matter what project you choose for a baby's or child's room, it should be one that gives you delight in making it. Approach these small projects with a spirit of playfulness and joy. Hooking something for a child you cherish makes that joy a given.

Addison's room décor includes the colors of gray, yellow, and white and the elephant motif. I chose two pillows to hook for the chair and a rug with Addison's name for the floor. Another item in the room is a quilt made by her other grandmother that adds a bright green to the color plan. I also added pink to round out the color palette.

Pattern provided on page 118

Addison's Rug, 32" x 22", wool on linen. Designed and hooked by Norma Batastini, Glen Ridge, New Jersey, 2018.

Elephant Pillow, 15" x 22", wool on linen with polyester stuffing. Designed by Heavens to Betsy and hooked by Norma Batastini, Glen Ridge, New Jersey, 2018.

Geometric Elephant Pillow, 15" x 22", wool on linen with purchased pillow form. Designed and hooked by Norma Batastini, Glen Ridge, New Jersey, 2017.

Jack's Rug, 32" x 22", wool on linen. Designed and hooked
by Norma Batastini, Glen Ridge, New Jersey, 2018.

Pattern provided on page 119

Eventually the baby grows and is ready for a bed, or maybe another baby is expected and the crib will be needed for the newborn. For Jack's "big boy" room, the main item is the switch to a real bed. At this age, cars and trucks are a big interest and the décor and bedding reflect that, as do the colors: blues, gray, orange, white, and a little yellow. The geometric pillow was hooked using these colors in a design that is more age-appropriate for a toddler and preschooler. I used many leftover strips from the pillow to hook the rug with Jack's name.

Choosing Your Materials

For wool selection, start by matching the actual colors being used in the room with paint chips or fabric swatches. To give interest and variety to your hooked piece, choose lots of wool in each colorway because by mixing solids, textures, and plaids, the piece will have movement and depth. Finding a plaid with all of colors in your plan would be a good way to tie everything together, but that may not be possible.

Sometimes there may be glints of colors not specifically in your color plan; you can still use these plaids as long as they are complementary to the overall look. Spot dyes also add interest, especially when mixed into background areas or large motifs. In this way you can expand your palette to include a range of tints and tones from all the colors in your piece.

For the youngest children, I prefer to keep it simple by using only wool and none of the embellishing fibers being used in hooking today. Save those touches for older children who aren't putting everything in their mouths!

After flirting with many styles of rug hooking, I've been infatuated by geometrics for the last several years, to the point that I really don't want to hook anything else! For me, the inherent structure of geometrics satisfies my need for order, while the simple shapes are ideal for playing with layers of color.

My Amazing Matrix series of rugs (modern inch mats featuring simple shapes created from a 1" grid) has evolved into a new series of free-form geometrics. And while my work naturally has a degree of uniformity, I am constantly reminding myself that it does not need to be perfect. Shapes don't have to be identical to be the same, nor do they need to be exactly symmetrical. The brain seems to autocorrect as needed.

For these latest rugs, I like to start hooking with only a basic idea for my design and a pile of colors I would like to use, allowing lots of room for both to evolve as my work progresses. Not really knowing exactly what I'm doing—and making it up as I go—is all part of the adventure. The overall appearance is constantly changing. I'm always curious to see how it is going to look, so I'm easily motivated to get to the very end so that I can know for sure! And as an added bonus, hooking

and filling in as you go means not struggling with a whole stretch of boring background to hook at the end!

I like to use small amounts of lots of different wools—and some of these can be quite subtle variations of one another. Switching a couple of brighter strips for lighter or duller ones can change the appearance of the overall color of different shapes, even if most of the wool used is the same! Without many variations in value (as well as in color), any pattern will easily become lost and a rug will probably look boring. For this reason, it's really important to have enough variety, and especially to make sure that you have an adequate balance of lights and darks.

I find that adding neutrals really makes colors sing. If you want to have an easier time integrating colors, it is best to steer away from a medium background. Instead, pick something light or dark, preferably a more neutral color. These geometric rugs also provide a great opportunity to mix in remnants from previous projects. (No piece is too small! Just try to keep to the same cut size; #8 is my favorite.) Not only does this help use up your stash, it also adds interest and a bit of the unexpected. (As an added bonus it also makes any (hopefully unnecessary) future repairs a lot easier and more forgiving!

A Pillow for Jack, 22" x 15", wool on rug warp backing with purchased pillow form.
Designed and hooked by Jen Manuell, Elmsdale, Ontario.

A pillow hooked in the colors of a little boy's room, yet still relevant when he is a man. The biggest challenge in hooking this pillow was to make each diamond unique, both in color and in design, while more or less creating the pattern on the fly on a blank piece of rug warp. Think rug hooking meets counted cross-stitch, but without a chart to guide you.

Inspiration for the Nursery

- Use motifs for the blocks on pillows or in a small alphabet rug with the name of the child.

- Hook animal shapes and back with black and white fabrics that will catch a newborn's eye. Hang these from a mobile, use them as curtain tiebacks, or display them on windowsills.

- Many small decorative items can be used as ornaments throughout a lifetime. Be sure to put the date and your initials on the back.

- Make pillows in all sizes using animal shapes. They are fun and appeal to all ages. Use motifs found in the nursery décor, or even use a pet as a model.

Copyright Thoughts

All of the children's items found in stores today are protected by copyright law. That includes bedding, clothing, toys, and other décor items that have been specifically designed for a particular store. Even though the items themselves might be discontinued after a season, the copyright lives on.

Let's use as an example a quilt with appliquéd animals in gray, white, and yellow. You can use the same colors that are in the quilt; copyright law does not protect colors. However, if the colors are used in a specific pattern or design, that arrangement cannot be copied because that is a designer's creative work.

Use your creativity and come up with ideas that coordinate well with the quilt, combining colors in new and interesting ways. Add textures and plaids for interest. Draw other animal motifs or change the style of the animals in the quilt; for example, think cartoon or primitive or contemporary or impressionistic. Visit copyright-free Internet sites if you are really stumped.

The Color Gray

Gray is a very popular color in home décor these days. It has replaced beige, ecru, and ivory as a backdrop for interiors. Classic gray gives a room a soothing, calm feeling. It mixes well with antique or contemporary living settings in casual or sophisticated styles. As rug hookers we are very familiar with the gray scale and the importance of value. Lighter grays seem more feminine while darker grays appear more masculine. Mix values to balance this effect.

As with all neutral colors, grays have a range of undertones that show through, including purple, pink, blue, and green. Use these undertones to your advantage when choosing a gray that works with the other colors you will be using in your project. Golden yellow would be enhanced with a gray that has purple undertones. Orange would be enhanced by a gray with blue undertones, and red with a gray that has green undertones. Consult a color wheel to see other possible combinations.

The gray wools I usually use are recycled skirts. Although some are heathery, when hooked they look very flat. For backgrounds or large motifs, mix several gray wools together to give some movement to the area. Add gray textures into your mix, as well as plaids that are predominantly gray. In the *Elephant Pillow* (page 8), I used many different gray wools and hooked the strips following the shape of the elephant. In *Jack's Rug*, I used a variety of gray wools for the inside background. After hooking the letters, I used the lightest gray to highlight and outline each letter. Then, in an echo style, I hooked each progressive row with a different gray. Like ripples in a pond, this created changes in color and value, giving the large background area much more interest.

The use of gray as a background can sometimes dull down a color plan, so include brighter colors in the motifs or other areas to offset this problem. Use strong contrast in the main motifs so they stand out. In *Jack's Rug* I first hooked the letters with orange and then outlined them with a strong navy blue. The first border has a light gray background, so the circle shapes include orange, yellow, and white for brightness. I used navy blue and gray for strong contrast. The hit-or-miss outside border includes all of the colors in the rug, thereby balancing the colors and values. I hooked the final border with dark blue, then a final row of navy. To finish, I whipped the edge with a gray yarn similar to the highlight row around the letters.

Chapter 2
Nursery Rhymes and Songs

> "Have you ever seen a baby bouncing up and down in the crib in time to some music? When you think of it, some of that baby's first messages from his or her parents may have been lullabies, or at least the music of their speaking voices."
> —Fred Rogers

Do you have memories of songs and nursery rhymes from your own childhood? If so, they probably quickly come to mind when you are soothing an infant or entertaining a young child. The words of lullabies are simple and easily repeated, with one or two main ideas. Their simplicity and gentleness create a peaceful mood, hopefully right before bedtime. The most familiar lullabies have been passed down for generations and have many different versions. With their simple ideas and comforting images, they are easy to convert to a rug design. If a particular lullaby has been used regularly in your family, a rug with that theme will have meaning for years to come.

Playing with an older infant or toddler is challenging, and this is where nursery rhymes come into play. Many rhymes have been put to music and have hand and arm movements to go along with them to act out the words of the song. Think of "Itsy Bitsy Spider" and "I'm a Little Teapot." Both are charming, with simple messages and simple images. Both are easy to translate into rug designs. "I'm a Little Teapot" is offered as a pattern.

Early songs are often used for educational purposes. In "Old MacDonald Had a Farm," children learn and imitate the sounds of farm animals. In "The Alphabet Song," they practice letters. These are great sing-along activities and offer lots of room for improvisation. They are also rich sources of rug ideas. Many commercial patterns feature ABCs and farm scenes. A classic example is *Alphapets*, by Muzzy Petrow. It is shown in this book both in a primitive style with soft colors and in a contemporary style with brighter colors. The design was developed in the 1990s and has been a classic, hooked by many through the years. You can personalize any design to fit the traditions and interest of your family.

Inspiration for Nursery Rhyme and Lullaby Rugs

- If your family has a favorite song or lullaby, use that as the start of a rug design. Include the words or images that quickly convey the meaning.

- Musical notes and symbols work well as a border.

- Popular lullabies: "Rock-a-bye Baby," "Twinkle, Twinkle, Little Star," and "Hush, Little Baby."

- Popular nursery rhymes: "There Was an Old Woman Who Lived in a Shoe," "Little Miss Muffet," "Little Boy Blue," "Baa, Baa, Black Sheep."

- Popular songs: "The Wheels on the Bus," "Itsy Bitsy Spider," "Mairzy Doats," "Old MacDonald Had a Farm."

Copyright Thoughts

Traditional lullabies have been handed down for generations, with many variations on the wording. They are not protected by copyright so you may use the words. The same is true of nursery rhymes that originated hundreds of years ago.

There are many current books of illustrated nursery rhymes. These illustrations are protected by copyright. Don't copy any image printed after 1923 without permission from the publisher.

Many children's songs being recorded by artists today have also been around for a long time. Do a quick Google search to check when a song was originally written to ensure you may use the words or related images without infringement.

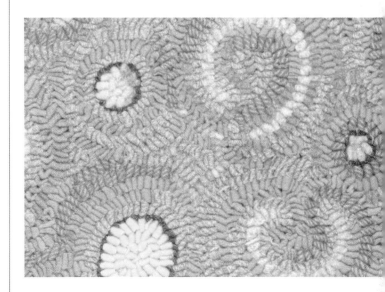

Froggie Went A-Courtin', 14" x 18", wool on linen. Designed by Norma Batastini and hooked by Mary Lou Bleakley, Arnold, Maryland, 2017.

"I hooked this rug for my great-grand because my mother sang the song to me, and I sang it to my children. My grandson had it played at his wedding and he sang it to his son. It was appropriate to hook the rug for his first child. The rug is based on an English ballad from the 1600s. It has been a popular song for Woody Guthrie, Pete Seeger, and Burl Ives. There are several different endings to the song, with the most kid-friendly being the version made popular by Burl Ives. The Bleakley family has our own version."

Humpty Dumpty

Humpty Dumpty sat on a wall,

Humpty Dumpty had a great fall.

All the king's horses and all the king's men

Couldn't put Humpty together again.

Humpty Dumpty, 11½" x 8", wool on linen. Designed and hooked by Kay Leisey, Mohrsville, Pennsylvania, 2018.

"I hooked this piece to bring to life a favorite nursery rhyme for my grandchildren. The biggest challenge was hoping Humpty would turn out looking like an egg. I tried to make his expression look surprised rather than hurt——no 'hurts' that Mommy can't fix for this guy! This English nursery rhyme comes from the 1800s."

Andrew's Alphabet Rug, 31" x 54", wool on linen. *Adapted from* Alphapets, *designed by Muzzy Petrow for Yankee Peddler Hooked Rugs and hooked by Lynn Volp, Huntington Bay, New York, 2018.*

"This rug was hooked for my grandson, Andrew, whose name is added to the A. He also requested a narwhal instead of a numbat. I was careful to not let the lion or tiger look too fierce. This was like hooking 26 rugs, which was tremendous fun."

Alpha Pets, 32" x 57", #8-cut wool on linen. Designed by Muzzy Petrow for Yankee Peddler Hooked Rugs and hooked by Linda Neary, Monroe Township, New Jersey, 2017.

Linda hooked this rug because she loves hooking animals and has a vision of how she wants each finished piece to look. Her challenge in this rug was to do every animal as though it was a separate rug of its own, giving each animal its own attention.

I'm a Little Teapot

Pattern provided on page 112

J'm a little teapot, short and stout.
Here is my handle, here is my spout.
When J get all steamed up, hear me shout.
Just tip me over and pour me out.

*I'm a Little Teapot, 21" x 20", wool on linen. Designed by Norma Batastini
and hooked by Denise Dondiego, River Edge, New Jersey, 2018.*

*"This was always a favorite nursery rhyme when my children were little and now I share it with
my first grandson. A collector of vintage teapots, I asked for the design to use the flower motifs from
a teapot in my collection on this rug. Each word was hooked with a different color of wool,
keeping your eye moving along as you sing the song. 'I'm a Little Teapot' is a familiar American
song written by George Sanders and Clarence Kelley in 1939. It became very popular and swept
the country."*

And Baby Makes Three, 31" x 65", assorted cuts of wool on linen. Designed and hooked by Judy Quintman, Wilmington, North Carolina, 2006.

Hooked for her seventh grandchild, Judy had family members join in and help with the hooking. Debbie Walsh, Gail Ferdinando, Julia Shaw, and Larry Quintman each did an animal. The motifs all have special meaning to this family.

Hey Diddle Diddle

Hey Diddle Diddle,
The cat and the fiddle,
The cow jumped over the moon.
The little dog laughed to see such sport.
And the dish ran away with the spoon.

The Cow Jumped Over the Moon, 20" x 33", wool on linen. Designed and hooked by Judy Quintman, Wilmington, North Carolina, 2009. FLiK Productions.

Judy generously hooked this to celebrate a friend's first baby. The blue hit-or-miss blocks create a playful background and work well with the bold motifs of the cow and moon.

Chapter 3

Biblical Stories and Myths

Family and faith are two of the most important elements in the life of the human race. Many of our holidays and rituals are centered on our religious beliefs. We come together at different times of the year to celebrate or observe these traditions. Usually they involve family and food. Many include special activities for children. It is a natural progression to use these special moments as a springboard for rug designs, especially as we decorate our homes for these occasions.

Our American culture has embraced many different religions, and today we more are familiar with the customs of many peoples throughout the world. This melting pot of ideas and beliefs includes Native American myths that are rich in imagery. This chapter will focus on biblical stories; some of these stories have entered into the wider culture and are familiar to all.

Noah's Ark is a well-known biblical story. The idea of a massive flood is also present in other religions. The story captures the imagination with its images of the animals embarking two by two, rain for forty days and forty nights, and a dove returning with an olive branch. Many famous artists have used this story as a theme for their paintings and drawings; view the work of Edward Hicks, Jan Brueghel the Elder, and Michelangelo. Contemporary artists have designed calendars, note cards, and decorative items around the Noah's Ark story.

Noah's Ark has also been very popular as a toy for children. The earliest versions were made in Germany, where children were allowed to play with them only on Sundays. Now antiques, these toys have become collectibles, and there are beautiful examples in private collections and museums. Often the animals were hand carved, with a variety of animals from all continents included. The lion, elephant, and zebra were the most popular.

Some artists have narrowed the field, using, for example, the animals of Africa or barnyard animals. Some ark sets include Noah and his whole family while others include only Noah and his wife. The style of the ark can be very simple, which was easiest for mass distribution. More elaborate arks reflect the architectural details important to the maker. All the ark sets include a ramp for the animals to walk up to enter the ark.

And the Rains Came Down, *25" x 21", wool plaids and textures on linen with cotton pockets. Adapted with permission by Norma Batastini from a Honey Bee Hive pattern and hooked by Janet Williams, Jefferson, Maine, 2016.* Impact Xpozures.

Janet spent a few years living in Africa, so she chose to change some of the animals. I love the gorilla! Janet used quilter's plastic templates for the animal shapes and to strengthen them. The pockets were made using a cotton fabric printed with animals.

And the Rains Came Down, *21" x 25", wool on linen. Adapted with permission from a Honey Bee Hive pattern and hooked by Norma Batastini, Glen Ridge, New Jersey, 2015.*

"As a new grandmother, I wanted this to be exciting and fun. While hooking the ark, the idea came to me to hook some three-dimensional animals that could be removed and played with. I added a row of pockets for the animals and attached it to the bottom of the finished rug. The wool for the pockets matched the wool binding all around the edge of the rug. I measured the bottom width of the rug, and chose five sets of animals that would complement the others in the rug design. They also had to fit into the pockets. The narrow alligator gave extra room for the wider elephants. This rug hangs in my guest room and is ready for any visiting child to enjoy."

Noah's Ark Sampler, 44" x 53", wool and silk on linen. Designed by Holly Hill Designs and hooked by Jan Levitt, Monroe Township, New Jersey, 2013.

Jan has a small collection of Noah's Ark pieces. She saw this iconic design and knew she had to hook it. An inventive and artistic rug hooker, Jan always personalizes commercial patterns.

Northern Noah, *33" x 30", wool on monk's cloth. Designed and hooked by
Ellen Savage, Pottstown, Pennsylvania, 2002.*

"These animals were quite challenging as I wanted them to be identifiable. They are all native to North America. The many different shapes and colors—as well as arranging each animal in the right position—kept this rug interesting to hook. Mr. and Mrs. Noah were fun to hook."

Noah and His Ark, 38" x 27", wool on linen. Designed by Norma Batastini
and hooked by Nancy Traficante, Rutherford, New Jersey, 2002.

*Noah is the prominent figure in a design layout that is similar to a sampler. The blocks of color around the edge
make an effective border.*

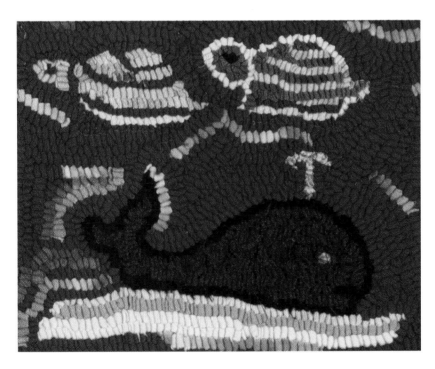

Artist's Statement: Cherylyn Brubaker

Because *Jack's Totem Family* is a children's rug, the design and colors chosen were paramount. In researching totem art, I was very drawn to the Pacific Northwest Coast Formline designs. They are beautiful and mostly red, black, and white. The designs are also very scary! They are quite fierce, with lots of teeth and sharp claws. Some of the animals are very abstract, their elements having been taken apart and rearranged. I spent many hours designing my totems from copyright-free images and photos and redrawing them in a Formline-inspired design that is hookable and "friendly." My initial drawings are pretty fussy and colored in red, black, and white. Perhaps these will be enlarged and hooked later. The totems I used on the mat design are simplified.

I wanted my rug design to be an imaginary scene one would see in a children's book. Incorporating the totem animals into a cohesive piece seemed to call for a landscape design. It was a natural to place the birds in trees. Drawing the salmon in the air moved it closer to the hawk and raven, eliminating the need for lots of water. The three totems are large; I made the trees smaller.

The colors of this rug are bright and colorful. All of the colors I used play off the initial hooking of Jack, the red-tailed hawk. The multi-green leaves on the trees were fun to hook, as was this whole adventure of *Jack's Totem Family* mat.

Jack's Totem Family, 25" x 28", hand-dyed and as-is wool on linen.
Designed and hooked by Cherylyn Brubaker, Brunswick, Maine, 2018.

"When my first grandchild was born, I knew I had to commemorate this joyous event. At the same time, I was working on presenting a class on personal totems. The animal symbols in this mat are the birth totems for Jack and his Mom and Dad. Jack is represented by the red-tailed hawk. Mom is the salmon and Dad is the raven. It took a bit of time to find the correct color for the background. The shade is more of a blue-violet than an aqua, created by mixing several values dyed over different base wools. I wanted the red-tailed hawk to stand out, so I hooked him first. I hooked the raven next, and he is deliberately not a dark black. The salmon is a combination of the colors of the hawk and the raven. It also made sense to pull the green into the lower quadrant of the mat."

Inspiration for Biblical Stories and Myths

- When presenting a rug based on a religious story or myth, purchase a book with that story as a companion piece and give them together.

- When designing a Noah's Ark rug, ask your children or grandchildren to draw some of the animals. It will engage them in the story and the finished rug.

- Explore Native American myths and artwork for unusual motifs representing North American flora and fauna.

- Add three-dimensional elements for added play opportunities.

Copyright Thoughts

Religious stories and myths are not protected by copyright; they were written centuries ago or have been handed down from one generation to the next. When designing, prepare by reading the original text. Study the work of the great master artists for composition and color ideas.

Contemporary (created after 1923) works of art depicting these stories cannot be copied without permission from the artist or publisher. Use them only for reference. Some designers like to see everything that has been done on a subject, while others don't want to see anything for fear of subconsciously copying. Use the method that is best for you without infringing on another artist.

Choosing and Using Color in Rugs for Children

Children love bright colors. A study posted by the National Institute of Health notes that children have positive responses to bright colors and negative responses to dark colors. When possible, consider using a brighter palette of colors when hooking for children. We react emotionally to the colors around us and each color has a special meaning.

- **RED** is the most emotionally intense color and is the color associated with love.
- **BLUE** is the most popular color and exudes a peaceful and calming atmosphere.
- **GREEN** symbolizes nature, is easy on the eye and is refreshing and energizing.
- **YELLOW** is cheerful, optimistic, and attention getting.
- **PURPLE** is romantic and sophisticated.
- **ORANGE** is warm, cheerful, and exciting.

As children grow into their teens, their color preferences change. They are influenced by the latest trends and the opinions of their peers. When hooking for older children, consult with them directly about their color preferences. Include them in the process and have gentle suggestions if their ideas won't work. Show them photos of hooked rugs so they have a better idea of the possibilities.

Working with bright colors can be challenging, especially if you usually work with a muted palette as I do. Here are a few tips:

- Not all of the colors used should be bright. Pick out the main motifs and make them bright so they become the focal point.

- Balance bright colors throughout the piece, choosing three or more places where each bright color will be used.

- Don't forget neutrals. They provide a place for the eye to rest.

- For maximum contrast, put a light and dark value next to each other.

- For less contrast, put medium-light and medium-dark values next to each other.

- Use spot-dyed wool and plaids to blend bright colors together.

Trust Me, 25" x 20", wool on monk's cloth. Designed by Norma Batastini and hooked by Cyndi Stinson, Westport, New Hampshire, 2018.

Daniel in the Lions' Den is a popular Bible story. Children love animals and they know how fierce lions are. They can grasp the power of God when they see Daniel unharmed. The lion designs evolved by pairs, each having their own color personality.

Pattern provided on page 113

Blessed Peace, *36" x 25", wool on linen. Designed by Norma Batastini and hooked by Nancy Traficante, Rutherford, New Jersey, 2004.*

"I wanted to portray a gentle-looking lion beside the baby lamb to emphasize the message of the story."

Moses in the Bull Rushes, 38" x 26", wool on linen. Designed by Norma Batastini and hooked by Nancy Traficante, Rutherford, New Jersey, 2001.

"The dark outlining gives the whole piece a stained-glass effect. Outlining the sections made it easy to hook. I love the contemporary look to the finished piece."

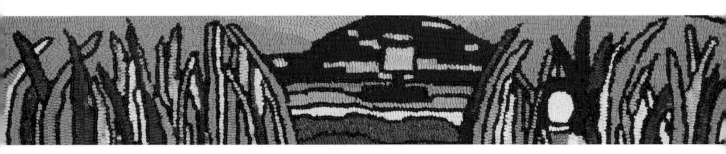

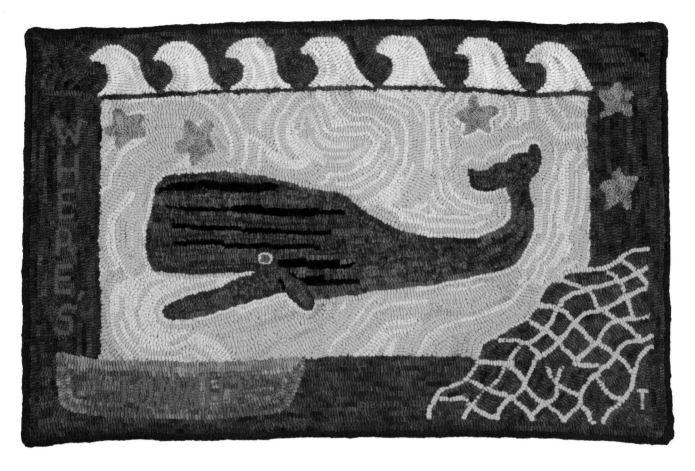

Where's Jonah?, 34" x 22", wool on linen. Designed by Norma Batastini and hooked by Nancy Traficante, Rutherford, New Jersey, 2008.

"Planning the border was really fun and makes the whole rug."

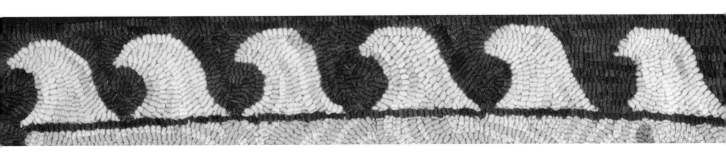

The Camel Who Knew the Way, *33" x 23", wool and decorative rayon ribbon on linen. Designed and hooked by Linda Woodbury, West Orange, New Jersey, 2017.*

"I like to have seasonal rugs everywhere, and hooking a camel seemed like a fun alternative to reindeer for the Christmas holiday. Working at a camp with Jule Marie Smith, I finished the left side and then put it away. Finally, in a 2017 class with Joan Reckwerdt, I added the village in the distance to the right side and the rug was finished. Using the rayon ribbon for the camel's blanket was difficult because it was very slippery and needed to be basted securely to keep it where it belonged."

3-D Animals, Dolls, and Toys

Now the fun begins—let's play! When a baby becomes a toddler, play becomes an important part of each child's day. Toys are supposed to be fun, but they are also an important part of a child's growth. Every toy offers some form of physical or mental development—sometimes both, as with the hooked ball, *Oh, Baby!* (page 44). The toddler will enjoy the physical activity of pushing the ball around and chasing after it. It offers the opportunity to play a simple game—rolling the ball back and forth from one child to another child or to an adult. On the educational side, the child can identify all of the motifs and learn new words and sounds.

There are several considerations as you decide what to make. The child's age and interests come first. Keep in mind that their interests change quickly. One week they love trains, the next week it's fire engines, and after that it's superheroes. Don't try to catch the current trend; make something that will have lasting interest. A child's age is a factor, too. A young child may not be old enough to use and understand all toys fully. For instance, a puppet portraying a character in a book may be beyond them, but they still may enjoy seeing the puppet on your hand, making gestures and "talking." Children have limitless imaginations and use them all the time in fascinating ways.

A basic toy can become many things depending on the child's stage of growth. Children often cycle back to toys they have seemingly outgrown. This is especially true when a younger sibling comes along. The outgrown farm set may once again have a lot of interest. A school-age child might want to read a story about a farm or teach the new sibling the barnyard sounds. Children look at toys from different perspectives at different stages and enjoy them in new ways.

Another consideration for grandparents is whether to send a handcrafted toy to the child's house or to keep it with you. Most children these days have an abundance of toys, and a treasured hooked toy may get lost in the bottom of the toy box. I have decided to keep toys at my house for special play when my grandchildren or children of friends visit—the hooked toys become a special experience and something they remember from their visits. It also solves the problem of having to make something for every child in a family—with large families this can become a burden. The first few items are fun, but then it can be hard to keep up!

Safety Concerns for Young Children

Choose your materials carefully so the toys you create are child-friendly and safe. Some small children put everything in their mouth and may even chew on toys when they are teething. Consider using natural fibers for the backing and the hooking. Wash all wool fabrics before hooking to remove excess sizing and finishes. Stuffing materials and batting are available in wool, cotton, and polyester and all are suitable. Some stuffing materials are labeled eco-friendly or organic, if that is important to you or the child's family.

Occasionally you may want to put some weight into an object so that is stands up independently. Do not use plastic pellets, metal balls, or coins. Natural products like sand, beans, or rice are a good alternative. For the farm animals, I made a muslin bag that would fit into the bottom of the animal and filled it with rice. The point is that if the hooked item opens up and the filling materials come out, they should be non-toxic if put in the mouth! Use a strong thread for sewing items together; I use a double strand of heavy-duty or quilting thread, which will stay strong when pulling together seams with the ladder stitch.

Toys and their parts should be large enough that they cannot be swallowed or lodged in the windpipe. If they can fit into a toilet paper roll they are too small. Decorative items, especially buttons, should not be used because they can come off and be swallowed. For instance, if you need an eye, appliqué a wool eye or hook the eye. Any string attached for a tail, hair, leash, etc., should not be longer than seven inches so it cannot be wrapped around the neck. Use your best judgment when deciding on materials and construction to make your hooked items safe. When in doubt, consult with the parents, who may have specific concerns about safety or will be up to date on the latest safety considerations.

Most hooked items can be cleaned easily with warm sudsy water using a mild dish detergent. Gently dab spots or lightly rub an entire area with the suds. Rinse with a cloth dampened with clear water. Let dry overnight. If loops are pulled or come out during normal use, they can be easily replaced. If the back of the piece is exposed or easily accessed, this is simple. I do not use any adhesives that would make repairs very hard or impossible. In one extreme disaster, my daughter and her friends spilled nail polish on her *Posey Cat* rug. After the polish dried, I removed the affected loops and hooked new strips in their place.

Let parents know how to clean items. When I give a hooked piece to a child, I want it to be used! Let parents know that a hooked piece can be repaired or cleaned. I would rather see that my gift has been played with, mellowed with use, and loved than remaining in perfect condition but never played with.

Design Thoughts for Older Children

For older children and teens, some of the precautions can be relaxed. They won't be chewing or swallowing the items you hook for them! Teens especially will respect a finished product that is purely decorative. They will appreciate the interest that alternative materials can give to hooked pieces. *Dragonfly* (page 86) is an example of a small piece with lots of interest. Beading, yarns, and silk strips add a more artistic and sophisticated look.

I have always loved geography and maps. Many manufacturers make floor rugs for children to use when playing with small cars and trucks. They often include houses, police and fire stations, hospitals, roads, and train tracks—a little miniature town. For a unique rug, hook your child's own town or a place they visit often. Include their house and those in their own neighborhood. Locate the main buildings of interest and place them in relation to other landmarks. Add their school, park or playground—all the places they know. When children grow older and are finished playing on it with cars and trucks, the rug will become a wonderful keepsake reminding them of where they grew up. A friend of mine who taught preschool recommended a rectangular shape rather than a square. On a longer, runner-shaped rug, the children do not have to climb onto the rug to reach the middle and maybe inadvertently knock over another playmate's vehicle.

The hooked example from Linda Woodbury (page 43) is the town where we both live. She has included all of the main buildings as well as both of our houses. Most of the town is a historic district, so Linda's design reflects those architectural details. For the hospital, which has been modernized, she retained the older look and the Red Cross symbol as identification. The town is long and narrow so it easily fit in the shape of a rectangle.

Farm and Animal Play Set, *barn is 18" x 12" x 12", animals of various sizes, mostly #3- and 4-cut wool on monk's cloth. Designed by Norma Batastini and hooked by Ellen Savage, Pottstown, Pennsylvania, 2018.*

"Mother and daughter teamed up to create the playset. I came up with the idea and drew the basic barn shape. Ellen hooked the barn and added details like the flowers and animals looking out the windows. She also designed all of the animals, refining them as she was hooking. I engineered the construction of the barn and added the roof. I spent many nights sewing a backing on each of the animals, stuffing them with fiberfill, and adding packets of rice for weight. As I was hooking I imagined all the kiddies playing with the animals and putting them away in the barn."

Raggedy Ann and Andy, *12" x 22", wool and yarn on linen. Designed by American Country Rugs and hooked by Norma Batastini, Glen Ridge, New Jersey, 2003.*

I love the Raggedy Ann and Andy stories and characters. This take-off on those characters with angel wings was a fun project. The dolls were backed with wool and stuffed with polyfil to make soft pillows. The hair was looped onto the hooking and backing after the dolls were sewn together.

Artist's Statement: Kathleen Donovan

Norma approached me a while ago with a proposition: She was writing a book on hooking for children and how would I like to try creating something new? How about hand puppets?

I do love a challenge—anything that stretches my brain—so after a bit I said I would try. We discussed some ground rules and I was off! First step was to choose a familiar fairy tale or nursery rhyme to portray. I read a lot of them before deciding on "The Owl and the Pussy-Cat," by Edward Lear. These were easily recognized characters that could be hooked in a straightforward presentation.

I then looked at pictures of manufactured puppets representing many different characters, just to give me some basic ideas. My first task was to choose a basic outline and the size. I wanted room for fingers—small enough for children but large enough for an adult to use with a child.

I started with the cat, adding hooked ears, a fun face, and tiger stripes. A rusty orange was chosen as a recognizable cat color and appealing to a child's eye.

Piggy came next. What else would do but a "dirty" piggy pink? Now it was time to play. I had to create a snout so he could have the ring in his nose, and so Piggy-Wig came to be.

Then came the owl. I chose a rusty brown to complement the cat, outlined in a dark brown overdyed with a bit of orange. I hooked accents in lighter yellows and gold wools. The overall effect was a convincing owl color and fun enough to appeal to children. The cut-out wool wing feathers flap quite nicely, adding even more fun.

What about stage props? I hooked a boat, guitar, honey pot, money bag, moon, and stars, as they were relevant to the story. I finished the flat ones like ornaments so they wouldn't curl and could be hung.

The puppets were great fun to create and I learned with each one. I enjoyed them so much that there are more ideas still floating about in my mind. I know I will be doing more in my future. Hmm . . . another nursery rhyme? A fairy tale? Maybe. Oh! How about a dragon?

The Pussycat, 10" x 9", dyed wool, felt, interfacing, and sewing thread on linen. Designed and hooked by Kathleen Donovan, Watchung, New Jersey, 2018.

"The hooked front of the cat is lined with felt that was applied with a lightweight iron-on interfacing. The back half of the puppet is wool dyed to match the front; it is cut slightly larger than the front. The bottom edge is folded up to the inside to form a hem, using the same iron-on interfacing to hold it in place. The backing wool is whip-stitched to the front, also catching the edge of the felt. This was the first puppet I hooked, and I learned a lot about the design and construction process."

The Owl, 11" x 15", dyed and as-is wool, cotton, and sewing thread on linen. Designed and hooked by Kathleen Donovan, Watchung, New Jersey, 2018.

"The front of the owl is lined with cotton that is cut slightly larger than the hooked front, then the edge is folded under so it matches the front and is basted in place. The back is a heavier-weight piece of wool. The beak was sculpted. Originally I wanted to use real feathers on the wings and as ear tufts, but I concluded they would be too fragile for children to play with, so I hooked the ear tufts. For the wing feathers I used layers of shaped wool scalloped at the bottom to appear feather-like and basted them in place. A separate strip of wool was glued across the shaped bottom, allowed to dry, and trimmed. The front of the owl is whip-stitched to the back, carefully going through all the layers on the wings."

Pattern provided on page 114

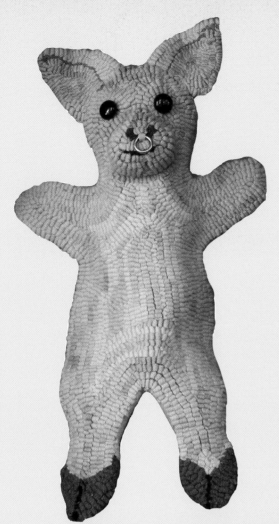

Piggy-Wig, 9" x 15", dyed and as-is wool, cotton, buttons, metal ring, fiberfill, wire, and sewing thread on linen. Designed and hooked by Kathleen Donovan, Watchung, New Jersey, 2018.

"This was my second puppet and I wanted to try something different, so why not a full-length body? I first increased the neck–shoulder angle for more flexibility, then added the bottom half of the body. During assembly, the backing was cut to cover the lower half of the body and stitched on the edges, then fiberfill was added inside the legs before the top edge was stitched in place. For the snout, I hooked the front piece, then a band to match the circumference. I sewed the band to the front snout piece and added a ring to the front between the nostrils. The snout was then stuffed with fiberfill and sewn onto the backing in the proper location on the face. I sewed on buttons for eyes and bent wire in shape to match the edges of the ears, then sewed the wire in place on the back of the hooking. I did this so the ears would have a cupped appearance.

Hooked on Puppets, 23" x 10½", recycled as-is wool on linen. Designed and hooked by Kathleen Donovan, Watchung, New Jersey, 2018.

"This piece was created to cover the front panel on the theater to make it more relevant to the hooking and more my own."

The Owl and the Pussy-Cat

The Owl and the Pussy-cat went to sea
In a beautiful pea-green boat,
They took some honey, and plenty of money,
Wrapped up in a five-pound note.
The Owl looked up to the stars above,
And sang to a small guitar,
"O lovely Pussy! O Pussy, my love,
What a beautiful Pussy you are,
You are! You are!
What a beautiful Pussy you are!"

- From The Random House Book of Poetry for Children, 1983.

Written by Edward Lear, a prolific writer and artist in 1871. A Londoner, he enjoyed writing nonsense poetry, this one for the child of a friend. Here is the first stanza. If you are not familiar with the entire work, be sure to look it up. It is a wonderful piece to recite with a child.

Inspirations for Toys

- Design a doll from a favorite photo of a child, using the child's facial features and hair color. Make clothes that match what the child was wearing.

- Design a rug and use motifs of a child's favorite toys.

- Make beanbags of all different sizes for indoor games.

- Make a stuffed animal based on a beloved pet.

Design generic dolls that can be used in imaginative play such as a princess, mermaid, superhero, villain, or witch.

Copyright Thoughts

There are many toy items that are generic such as a ball, stuffed animal, car, truck, or puppet. These items have been made for generations and are not protected by copyright. Be careful not to copy products or specific design elements from toy manufacturers or other companies making merchandise for children.

For example, my children and grandchildren have played with a Fisher-Price farm set, an iconic toy in our family. But farm sets themselves have been around for years, and many versions from early toymakers in Germany are collectibles today.

When I decided to create a hooked version, I did not copy the Fisher-Price version. I chose my own size, details, and colors. My mother, Ellen Savage, hooked it and embellished the barn with animals looking out the windows. She also hooked a pitchfork, shovel, and flowers along the bottom edge. We finished the animals by stuffing and weighting them for easy play.

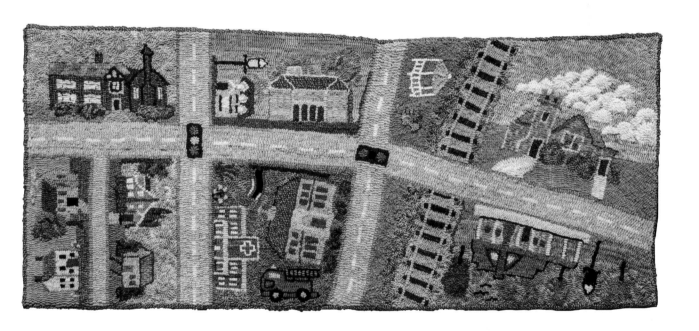

Glen Ridge, My Hometown, 48" x 19", wool on linen. Designed and hooked by Linda Woodbury, West Orange, New Jersey, 2018.

"Simplify, simplify, simplify! Hooking the buildings in my town became an architectural study of perspective and relationships. Making the rug appropriate for children's activities necessitated reducing the size and details of each structure. My biggest technical problem was making the parallel sides of the train tracks stay even when I wasn't hooking on the straight grain of the backing. I persevered and captured the essence of the tracks and the watery glen, the historic train station, the schools my son attended, our municipal building, the local hospital, and my church. Of course, my home and my friends' homes are included. I envision myself on the floor, sharing stories about our family in Glen Ridge with future grandchildren, and driving trucks and cars all over the rug."

My friend Vicki Simpson, of Bath, Maine, makes beautiful and meaningful baby balls to celebrate the birth of her friend's children and now grandchildren. She has an amazing collection of cotton fabrics with such a variety of themes printed on the material. When a child is born, she knows the colors and likes of the family and matches it with her fabrics to create a very personal baby ball.

Because I like collaborative projects, I asked Vicki to make a baby ball with her favorite fabrics. She picked themes that included music for her husband Hank, who plays the trumpet, son John who lived in Tokyo, daughter Julia who loves elephants, cactus for her time in Tucson, kids holding hands for our long friendship, a snow scene for the dramatic Maine winters, a sail boat and other personal stories.

I adapted all the designs to make them my memories, too. In 2016, the Green Mountain Rug Hooking Guild challenge was to hook a piece for a child, and that is how *Oh, Baby!* was born.

I'm so happy that Norma's grandchildren now are playing with this giant ball.

Cotton Baby Ball, *made by Victoria Simpson, owned by Norma Batastini.*

"I used this ball as an inspiration and model for my hooked and braided ball, Oh, Baby!*"*

Oh, Baby! *18" diameter, wool on linen. Designed, hooked, and braided by Kris McDermet, Dummerston, Vermont, 2016.*

"I hooked this piece as part of a challenge, to hook a three-dimensional piece. It was modeled after the fabric balls that young children play with and has a bell inside. The challenge of this piece was to get each section just the right size so that everything would fit when sewed together. After the show I gave the ball to Norma Batastini for her grandchildren."

Bunny Sign, *bunny: 22" x 34"; flags: 12" x 17". Wool on linen mounted on wooden board. Designed and hooked by Judy Quintman, Wilmington, North Carolina, 2011.*

Judy designed this piece to delight her grandchildren when they visit. She thought it would be fun to change the flag for holidays, birthdays, or special occasions. It can be used inside or outside in a sheltered area.

Valentine's Day Flag

Thanksgiving Flag

Welcome Flag

The Games We Play

Playing games is a favorite pastime for children of all ages. Why not hook a game board? There are many traditional games to choose from—checkers, chess, backgammon, Chinese checkers, tic-tac-toe, and Parcheesi come to mind. There are commercial patterns available with these designs but it is easy to transfer them onto backing yourself. Personalize your design with motifs or designs that have meaning to you and your family. In *Checkerboard Cats*, Ellen Savage added cats at each end of the board to represent the family cats through the years.

Checkerboard Cats, 34" x 18", wool on monk's cloth. Designed and hooked by Ellen Savage, Pottstown, Pennsylvania, 2006.

"All of these cats, over the years, have lived in my house. I mostly claim these cats as mine because I was the one who fed and cared for them. They were mainly cats dropped off and rescued, and they actually 'belonged' to my children. I selected the colors in this piece to resemble each of our cats."

Some game boards are hooked to be decorative only, but others are intended to be used. The question comes up as to what to use for the game pieces. Often you can purchase game pieces separate from the boards. Craft stores sell generic game pieces that can be stained or painted to match the colors in the hooking. In *Tic-Tac-Toe*, Sandy Francisco hooked her own Xs and Os. The size of the board, 24" x 24", is large enough that it was possible to hook the pieces in a size that would fit into the squares. For some games, the pieces would need to be so small that hooking them would not be an option. When designing your game board, consider how it will be used, the size, and whether game pieces can be made or need to be purchased.

Many children are involved with sports during their childhood. Little tots start kicking a soccer ball. T-ball sets are available for three-year-olds. Infants take swimming lessons. Physical activity at school and after school is encouraged as children spend more and more time with electronics. Team sports engage children socially as well as building cooperation skills and friendships. The commitment of time and money is great, so sports become an important part of our lives.

Rugs designed around a sporting activity will have lasting memories. I designed *Let's Play Ball* for my grandson. From an early age he was attracted to anything with a ball. The design includes all types of balls—including some that he has not been introduced to yet. I wanted a design that would appeal to him for a long time. I even added hockey pucks because that is a sport he loves, too.

Let's Play Ball, 24" x 36", #4 - and #6- cut wool on linen.
Designed by Norma Batastini and hooked by Ingrid Hieronimus, Ontario, Canada, 2018.

This rug was designed to give the impression that the balls had just dropped on it randomly. Of course, there was some planning to balance out the colors. The large balls were hooked in over dyed textures in realistic colors. Solid black was used for outlining, but a dyed black (Multiple Fusion Spot #1) was used for filling in larger areas. The white balls were either natural or white. This design could be personalized to use the balls or sporting equipment your child enjoys. Consider a border with other sports equipment—bats, sticks, mitts. Team logos, teammates' names, and team colors could also be incorporated.

Other school activities may inspire a rug: think about cheerleading, chorus, band and orchestra, debate team, and drama clubs. Many of these activities involve hours and hours of time commitment for the student and the parents.

Many families have a long tradition of team fandom, passed from one generation to the next. Why not use team logos and slogans that we see plastered everywhere? Be aware, though, that these are not free to use without restriction; they are copyright protected by the leagues and teams. Our family's passion is baseball—the New York Yankees. I hooked a rug celebrating the Yankees for my son as a college graduation gift. Major League Baseball allows for a one-time use of its logos. (See Copyright Thoughts, page 52 .) Most professional leagues and colleges have similar policies, but check first to be certain you are adhering to their rules.

New York Yankees, 34" x 20", wool on linen. Designed and hooked by Norma Batastini, Glen Ridge, New Jersey, 2006.

We are a baseball family and the Yankees are our team (although with my son's marriage we now have some Red Sox fans in-house too!). I hooked this rug for my son to remember all the fun times we had at the games during their incredible championship run. I have extra wool stashed away so I can change the numbers when they win another World Series!

Tic-Tac-Toe, 24" x 24", wool on linen. Designed by Norma Batastini and hooked by Sandy Francisco, Little Falls, New Jersey, 2017.

Sandy plans to keep this piece at her home to use at family gatherings where all four grandchildren can enjoy it.

Pattern provided on page 115

Artist's Statement: Marsha Moyer-Payne

Because Taryn is a very engaged girl, I wanted to make a piece she could interact with, not just an art piece. She is also curious and loves animals. Wow, a hopscotch board made of lily pads, not just squares! The lily pads would be set in a stream. Along the way, she could encounter some fanciful creatures. (From the bottom, an iguana, a duck, a frog, a turtle, a swan, and three colorful fish.) Proddy flowers with color and beautiful petals from my imagination could do the trick.

I added dimension with the Waldoboro technique, used to enhance cattails, a flower, and a lily pad. The biggest challenge was the stream—showing movement and enclosing it all. When I give this to Taryn, she will decide whether it should hang on the wall or remain on the floor, all ready for some hopping. Painted flat rocks will be used by the players, reminding them of skipping stones.

Taryn's Rug, 23" x 68". Designed and hooked by Marsha Moyer-Payne, Medford, New Jersey, 2018.

"A popular childhood activity is playing hopscotch. Drawing the hopscotch outline on the sidewalk with chalk is a rite of growing up, especially for girls."

I wanted to create a rug for my daughter Madelin that would represent a part of who she is and what she loves, so I designed a rug that represents her love of cheerleading. I had several challenges just coming up with the design but opted for this simple and fun cheerleader surrounded by hearts and stars that lovingly surround her name and the hometown she cheers for. I asked Madelin for her input on the colors and she said, "Mom, just keep it simple!" I used blues and whites that represent her team colors and the lavender hues that matched her new and freshly-painted room. Several challenges came up as I was designing and hooking the rug. The first was the type and placement of the lettering; I finally decided to blend the words at the letter E. The stars also posed some problems. I rehooked them a few times and finally opted for an unperfected look. (Are stars really perfect looking, anyway?) The face was challenging, and I decided to make her face simple and sweet in keeping with a naive look. Hooking this piece was a time of love and, best of all, Madelin is very pleased with it.

Maddie's Rug, 36" x 45", wool on linen. Designed and hooked by Kirsten O'Connor, New Jersey, 2018.

Inspiration for Game Rugs

- Make beanbags. They can be used for many games and are good for development of gross motor skills.

- Design a rug with a child's high-school activities.

- Make pillows in their favorite ball shape—round shapes are the easiest.

- Don't forget uniforms. The shapes, colors, and uniform number can be used in a border design.

- Write a story or description of the activity and tuck it into a special pocket sewn on the back of the rug. Little details can be forgotten over time but will stay in the rug pocket for future generations.

Semper Fi Patriotic Checkers, 22" x 22", wool on linen. Designed by Polly Minick and hooked by Sandy Francisco, Little Falls, New Jersey, 2010.

Sandy hooked this for her first grandchild, Thomas. It was given as a rug to be used, and Thomas likes to play checkers with his friends.

Copyright Thoughts

The big game makers are protective of their products. Here is a summary of what the US Copyright Office has to say about games:

Copyright does not protect the idea for a game, its name or title, or the method or methods for playing it. Nor does copyright protect any idea, system, method, device, or trademark material involved in developing, merchandising, or playing a game. Once a game has been made public, nothing in the copyright law prevents others from developing another game based on similar principles. Copyright protects only the particular manner of an author's expression in literary, artistic, or musical form.

Material prepared in connection with a game may be subject to copyright if it contains a sufficient amount of literary or pictorial expression. For example, the text matter describing the rules of the game, or the pictorial matter appearing on the game board or container, may be registrable.

Therefore, it's best to assume that the graphics used on the board, including motifs and color arrangements, are protected by copyright. Some games also have trademarks that protect brand names, slogans, and logos. A trademark can last forever if a game is in continuous use. For example, Monopoly is a trademark of Parker Brothers. The artwork of the game is copyrighted. Permission to use either must be obtained to avoid violating the law, even by making a hooked rug for personal use.

When planning to use logos or slogans of professional sports teams or colleges and universities, first learn about their policies. When hooking a New York Yankees rug, I found the following information on the MLB website. This policy covers all of the teams in the league:

The MLBAM Properties are either owned by or licensed to MLBAM. The applicable owners and licensors retain all rights to the MLBAM Properties, including, but not limited to, all copyright, trademark or other proprietary rights, however denominated. Except for downloading one copy of the MLBAM Properties on any single device for your own personal, non-commercial home use, you must not reproduce, prepare derivative works based upon, distribute, perform or display the MLBAM Properties without first obtaining written permission of MLBAM or otherwise expressly set forth in the terms and conditions of the MLBAM Properties. The MLBAM Properties must not be used in any unauthorized manner. — Major League Baseball Advanced Media

It is important to note that they specify Properties are to be used for personal and non-commercial use.

Old Parcheesi Board, *23" x 23", dyed and as–is wool on linen. Designed and hooked by Gail Ferdinando, Pittstown, New Jersey, 2018.*

"I've always loved the geometric designs of old game boards, and the colors of this one really appealed to me. The most challenging part of hooking it was keeping the large circles really round. I'm planning to hook some more game boards and make a series."

Chapter 6

Story Time

Books are a big part of a child's life. From board books, which are easy for little hands to hold and turn the pages, to storybooks for toddlers, children love being read to and talking about books. Story time becomes part of the bedtime ritual and an aid to get children to sleep at night. These favorite stories are great resources for rug-design ideas.

As children grow and begin reading on their own, novels like the *Harry Potter* series become popular. Movies and related merchandise are available for many stories. Use these items as inspiration but do not copy! For example, in the *Harry Potter* books, the owl Hedwig is an important part of the story. Draw your own owl or choose one of the many commercial owl patterns that are available. Personalize a purchased pattern with an added border and use colors that are used in the story.

Many contemporary stories are derived from literary traditions dating as far back as the Greeks. These stories do not have copyright protection, so you are free to use them in your rug-hooking projects. See Copyright Thoughts (page 57) for specifics about how to use the stories. *Grimms' Fairy Tales* were first published in 1812 with 86 stories. Jacob and Wilhelm, German brothers, published a seventh edition in 1857 with 211 fairy tales. They enjoyed great success and the stories spread throughout the world. Their fairy tales have been a source of inspiration for artists, writers, and composers. "Hansel and Gretel," "Cinderella," "Rumpelstiltskin," and "Bremen Town Musicians" are just a few of these tales.

Aesop was a slave and storyteller living in ancient Greece. His stories were originally for adults, but after the Renaissance they were used as educational materials for children. Each fable has a moral lesson explained through a colorful story. They were passed down in oral tradition long before the introduction of printing. Some of Aesop's well-known fables include "The Tortoise and the Hare," "The Boy Who Cried Wolf," and "The Fox and the Grapes."

Hans Christian Andersen published over 300 fairy tales in the 1800s. A Danish author, he started writing down the stories he had heard as a child. Some of his popular tales include "The Little Mermaid," "The Emperor's New Clothes," "The Ugly Duckling," and "The Snow Queen." They have inspired ballets, films, and plays.

Perhaps thinking about these stories will inspire you to hook a rug depicting the favorite story of a child in your life!

Whatever the story, whatever rug you make, you also have a story to tell about your rug! It's important to label all rugs for historical record as well as to remember the details about your rug. How often have you forgotten the name of a pattern or the year you hooked it? When you are hooking a rug for a child, include the usual information: pattern name, your name and address, and the date completed. For added interest, add details about whom you hooked the rug for and why. Include any information about your feelings about the rug or the child you are making it for. Note any special techniques or materials used.

Froggie, 30" x 20", #4-cut wool strips on rug warp. Designed by Prairie Craft House and hooked by Norma Batastini, Glen Ridge, New Jersey, 2014.

"I found this frog design in a box of old rug-hooking supplies that had been given to me by a rug hooker's now-elderly daughter who was cleaning out the attic. Under a stack of old burlap patterns was this wonderful frog. The frog was already hooked and I couldn't part with him. After giving him a thorough cleaning, I hooked the lily pads and background. I made a few changes to the frog to add more contrast. When my grandson was born, this piece seemed just right for a big pillow."

Artist's Statement: Debbie Walsh

My daughter Maggie's love of Alice in Wonderland was the deciding factor in what to hook for a class with Capri Boyle Jones at the 2017 Hunterdon County Rug Artisans Guild rug school. After brainstorming several rug layouts, my sister, Gail Ferdinando, came up with the scene that I chose; it included five of John Tenniel's original characters from *Alice's Adventures in Wonderland*. I printed out the drawings of the characters to be used in the rug and traced over them with pencil to simplify the details for hooking. Once I decided what size the rug should be, I got a piece of paper that was half that size. I drew the background details, including the hills and tree trunk, on a large sheet of paper. Then I used a copy machine to enlarge the characters in different sizes and placed them on the rug to determine which size to use for each. My daughter helped me come up with the words in the tree, "We are all mad here," from the book.

Once I had everything printed and laid out the way I wanted it, I taped the characters down and brought the whole thing to an office supply center to make a full-size copy of the design. I placed a piece of red dot transfer material over this copy and traced the design with pen. I laid this on a piece of linen and traced over the design with a black marker.

To color plan the rug, I put together a bag for each character with the colors I would use, plus a bag of greens for the leaves and hills, and one of browns for the tree trunk.

I started by hooking Alice. Capri helped me put several greens together for the leaves, which I hooked in irregular ovals, and we picked other greens to distinguish between the two hills. Capri dyed several blues for me to use in the sky and helped me to determine where each of the blues should go. I added some purples and gray tweeds to the tree trunk to get the look of a rough, knotty bark.

I really enjoyed hooking this rug, and I'm happy that Maggie is pleased with the way the rug turned out.

Alice in Rugland, 35" x 47". *Adapted from illustrations by John Tenniel. Designed by Debbie Walsh and Gail Ferdinando and hooked by Debbie Walsh, Cranford, New Jersey, 2018.*

Inspiration for Story Rugs

- Make the character in a favorite book as a stuffed toy or pillow.

- Make a hooked book as a keepsake. Combine hooking, embroidery, wool appliqué, and other techniques to tell a story.

- Have the child draw their favorite characters for a small rug.

- Children write short stories and poetry as school assignments, sometimes accompanied with pictures they have drawn. Design a rug around one of these with the child's input.

Copyright Thoughts

When designing a rug around a story, review the book's copyright page to make sure you are following the rules. Storybooks are usually lavishly illustrated, with many different artists and authors giving us beautiful images. If published after 1923, do not copy these images. Use alternative sources and create your own design. For instance, my son loved the Frog and Toad books by Arnold Lobel. When my grandson was born, I purchased the books and hooked the commercial pattern, *Froggie*, and made it into a large pillow perfect for lounging and reading.

The Walt Disney Company has adapted many fairy tales into successful animated movies. *A Bug's Life* is from Aesop, *Frozen* and *The Little Mermaid* are from Hans Christian Andersen, *Snow White and the Seven Dwarfs* is from the Grimm brothers. All these movies are accompanied by a vast array of merchandise to augment the experience, but the basic stories are in the public domain. If a child wants a particular character in the gift you are hooking, draw a few variations or have the child draw a picture of the character. Engage them in the process and explain that film characters cannot be copied, just as the child's own drawings are protected by copyright as soon as they make them. (See Commonsense Thoughts about Copyrights Rules for Rug Hookers, page 4.)

Pattern provided on page 118

1 *I Think I Can,* 40" x 12", wool on linen. Designed by Norma Batastini and hooked by Sandy Francisco, Little Falls, New Jersey, 2006.

"I made this design for Sandy as a thank you for a big favor she had done for me. Her grandson, Thomas, had just been born, so I knew a train would be a good subject."

2 *I Think I Can,* 42" x 12", wool solids and textures on linen. Designed by Norma Batastini, with additions by Liz Marino, and hooked by Nancy Lamoureaux, Pittsfield, Massachusetts, 2016.

"It was a wonderful challenge to make this wall hanging for my two youngest grandchildren, Camden and Alaina. The words, animals, and people, were designed by Liz Marino. It has a perfect home in my grandchildren's play area." Jane McWhorter.

3 *I Think I Can,* 42" x 16", wool on linen. Designed by Norma Batastini, with additions by Liz Marino, and hooked by Robbin Halfnight, Housatonic, Massachusetts, 2018.

"I originally began hooking this rug for my grandson but another baby boy came along before it was finished, so it became a rug for both Kai and Theo. I added the Canadian flag because my family has dual citizenship." Jane McWhorter.

4 *I Think I Can,* 42" x 12", wool solids and textures on linen. Designed by Norma Batastini, with additions by Liz Marino, and hooked by Barbara Belmonte, East Canaan, Connecticut, 2017.

"I hooked this rug for my great-grandson, Jackson, for the wall in his bedroom. I enjoyed adding the words, animals, and people that really makes the rug come alive." Jane McWhorter.

5 *Oh, The Places You'll Go,* 42" x 16", hand dyed wool on linen. Designed by Norma Batastini and hooked by Christine Dube, Williamsburg, Virginia, 2016.

"My grandson Patrick's room has the theme of Dr. Seuss. I adapted the pattern to include the balloons and the familiar Dr. Seuss saying. The colors complement the ones used to decorate his room."

The Three Bears, 30" x 20", wool on linen, with a sliver of silver sparkle for the hot bowls of porridge.
Adapted from an antique pattern and hooked by Pat Hiller, Rutherford, New Jersey, 2015.

"I hooked this rug for my grandson, Will, who enjoys hearing the story. Hooking the bears was the most fun, especially spiffing up their outfits."

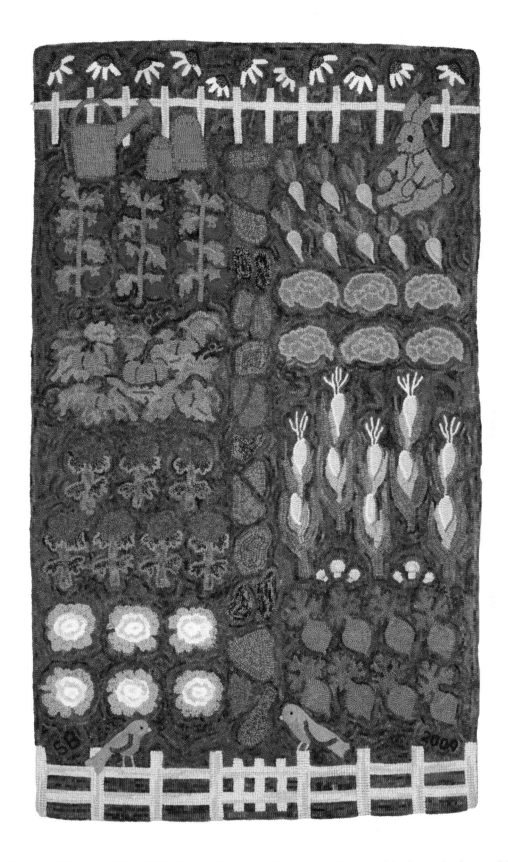

Mr. McGregor's Garden, *36" x 60", #6- and 8-cut wool on linen. Designed by Patsy Becker and hooked by Sandy Bennington, Old Tappan, New Jersey, 2009.*

"I first saw this rug on the cover of the ATHA magazine in 2001, the year I started hooking. I loved it, remembering the story from my own childhood. I still have that book. I was determined to hook the rug someday, and I started it in a class with Patsy Becker in 2004. Now I am reading the story again to my grandchildren."

Chapter 7

Children's Art

The artwork of young children is not bound by rules. They express their thoughts freely, using motifs and colors in an original way to tell a story. For a child, art is spontaneous, experimental, and a form of play. It is also a means for them to communicate ideas and feelings that they may not be able to express with words. The results are charming and have a naiveté that evokes emotional response. Some drawings are reminiscent of the primitive hooked rugs that we love.

The artwork of older children, especially those in high school and college, is more sophisticated. With art classes, they learn basic principles of composition and use more complex color combinations. Drawings and paintings are more stylized, with specific structure. Their work usually has a deeper meaning and an intentional message they are trying to impart. These pieces are equally suitable for rug hooking, especially if you want a more contemporary look. *Cowboy* (page 69) and *Paintbrushes Pillow* (page 66) are two examples.

When choosing a child's artwork to convert to a rug-hooking pattern, consider the basic elements of visual art:

- Line—one point to another, drawn or implied. Lines move the eye around the work.

- Shape—a specific, confined area, limited in height and width. It can be two-dimensional or flat.

- Form—three-dimensional object, including height, width, and depth. Includes pyramids, cubes and spheres.

- Value—the lightness or darkness of colors.

- Color—the hue, value, and intensity of a color.

- Texture—how the surface area appears; for example, rough or smooth.

Consider the total composition. How are the elements of the design arranged? Is the arrangement pleasing to your eye? Surprisingly, most children's artwork adheres to these elements that they must intuitively sense. Some artwork may not adhere to all of these principles but nevertheless have a unique, quirky look that is appealing.

Often it is our own memories of our child's school days that make a work meaningful. When I started hooking *Noel, Noel* (page 65), my daughter was in the middle school. She had no memory of the drawing she had made for an assignment in second grade. She was somewhat embarrassed and asked me not to make it into a pattern for anyone else. Now an adult, she finds the drawing and rug charming. But it will always be more my memory than hers.

Another twist on this theme is the use of a parent's artwork for a child's rug. Two examples are *Melina's Parade* and *Oliver's Parade* (page 70). Their father is a photographer and made a series of whimsical photos with toy animals pulling vehicles. Lea McCrone adapted them to make a small piece for each of his children.

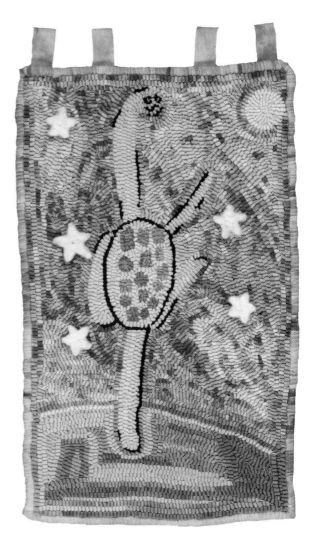

Dancing Giraffe, 13" x 21", wool and felted roving on linen. Adapted from the artwork of her granddaughter, Stella Flannery, and hooked by Sally Livingston, Glen Rock, New Jersey, 2012.

"My granddaughter made a watercolor of a dancing giraffe in kindergarten. He was so charming my daughter had it put on a T-shirt for Stella to give her dad on Father's Day. Giraffes are a favorite of mine. I wanted to hook him the minute I saw the painting, and I wanted to make it exactly like the picture. The hooking went smoothly except for the stars; they didn't stand out. I felted roving into the shape of stars and sewed them on. The mat now hangs on my back door, where all my grandchildren can enjoy it."

Artist's Statement: Norma Batastini

Noel, Noel was started over 20 years ago. I was new to rug hooking and wanted to learn everything. Projects piled up and went unfinished. Last year, I started working on this rug again.

The design was adapted from a drawing my daughter made in the second grade. The original drawing was 5" x 8", but I wanted to experiment with #8.5 and hand-cut strips, so the pattern had to be large. The original was a line drawing with no color, so I had to plan the colors.

I enlarged the drawing to 31" x 46" and chose vibrant colors for the children's clothes. The center figure was dressed in pink and purple, my daughter's favorite colors at the time she made the drawing. The blue-gray sky was hooked in circles, echoing out from the three children and the snowflakes. Because the theme was Christmas, I used red and green in the border and lettering, a cheerful addition that balances the children's clothing. One addition: I added my daughter's name, Meredith, at the bottom. I found an old school paper where she had written her name and enlarged it to fit the space. I used blue from the sky for the lettering, creating a subtle touch that doesn't take away from the bold lettering at the top.

Although I started out with a very wide cut of wool, I found it difficult to hook. (The backing is monk's cloth and doesn't have as much give the linen I use now.) Some wool I had already cut, but anything newly cut was cut narrower, in a #8 cut or #6 cut. The wide wool was perfect for the red curly line all around the edge. I outlined the children and the snowflakes (small circles) with a #5 cut in dark blue for emphasis. The background behind the words *Noel, Noel* I hooked horizontally as a contrast to the circles in the blue-gray sky. The children's faces were kept primitive in the spirit of the original drawing.

Most of the fabrics I originally started with were recycled wool pieces in solids, plaids, and textures. When I ran out of a particular color, I mixed in some new off-the-bolt or hand-dyed pieces. My favorite parts of the rug are the blond hair on the middle child, the red curlicue line, and the tall hats on the children.

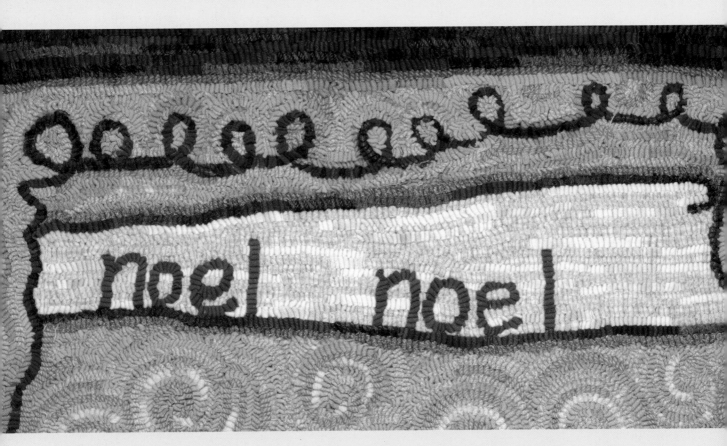

Noel, Noel, *31" x 46", wool on monk's cloth. Adapted from the artwork of Meredith Batastini and hooked by Norma Batastini, Glen Ridge, New Jersey, 2018.*

At the time this drawing was made, we were reading a lot of Dr. Seuss books to Meredith. The Seuss characters inspired the tall hats on the children.

Color photo.

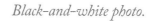
Black-and-white photo.

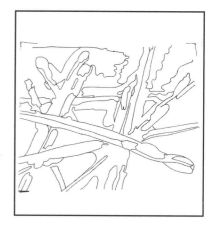

Tracing from the
black-and-white verison.

Paintbrushes Pillow, *19" x 22", hand-dyed #5-cut wool on monk's cloth. Adapted from the artwork of Joshua Kislevitz and hooked by Nara De Alcantara, Edgewater, New Jersey, 2017.*

"Joshua is a young man I cared for during his childhood. As a college student, Joshua made this painting for his father as a birthday gift. When I saw it, I loved the design and unusual colors. I asked Joshua if I could make a pillow of his painting. It was challenging to get the colors just right."

Enlarging and Transferring Patterns

This is how I enlarged *Paintbrushes Pillow*:

- I received a color photo, good for color planning.

- I copied the photo into black and white. For the drawing, I needed to be able to see the light and dark shadows as well as the main lines.

- On the black-and-white copy, with a fine marker I traced along the edges of every value, focusing on shapes, not worrying about color or design,

- I covered the black-and-white copy with tracing paper and traced the same lines again. This became my pattern.

- I enlarged the pattern to the size I needed for the pillow.

- I transferred the design to the rug backing. (Use the method you prefer: light table, red dot, or netting.)

Note: I do not enlarge the original photo to the size I want the rug to be. Photos can distort when they get bigger if not taken with a professional camera. I enlarge the photo to about 8½" x 11", for ease of drawing, and usually distortion is minimal at this size.

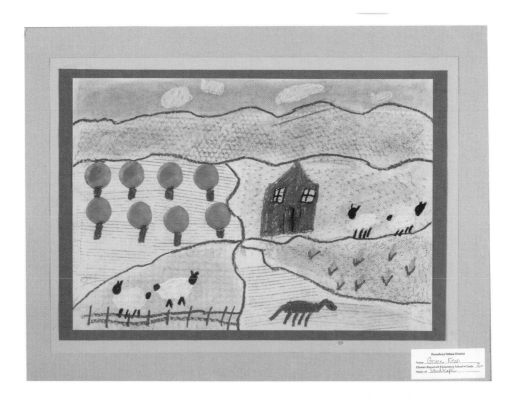

***Grace's Farm,** 25" x 17", wool on linen. Adapted from the artwork of her granddaughter, Grace Elizbeth Kean (at age eight), and hooked by Debi Roeder, Wykoff, New Jersey, 2015.*

"Grace's class was told to draw a farm with animals. When I saw Grace's drawing in pastels, I was taken by the Rufus Porter look. And the primitive style is just what I love to hook."

Cowboy, 32" x 39", wool on linen. Adapted from the artwork of her grandson, Blair Whiteford, and hooked by Joan Whiteford, Pompton Plains, New Jersey, 2010.

"My grandson studied art at Ringling College for Art & Design in Florida. He is now furthering his art studies at Yale University. I loved his use of color and adapted the painting for a rug in a class taught by Michele Micarelli."

The inspiration: the photo of a toy parade. "My youngest son's best friend is a photographer. Years ago he created a still–life parade with toy animals lashed onto vehicles. With his permission I hooked these pieces for his children. The original image is black and white, so I had complete freedom to bring the rugs into full color."

Melina's Parade, *28" x 10", dyed wool on monk's cloth. Adapted from the artwork of Brandon James and hooked by Lea McCrone, Malvern, Pennsylvania, 2014.*

Oliver's Parade, *28" x 10", dyed wool on monk's cloth. Adapted from the artwork of Brandon James and hooked by Lea McCrone, Malvern, Pennsylvania, 2017.*

Out on the Boat, *11" x 16", wool on linen. Adapted from the artwork of Catherine Mulcahy (at age four) and hooked by Beverley Mulcahy, Paxton, Massachusetts, 1996.*

"I enlarged a very small drawing by Catherine of our little family and dog on boating outing. (We never owned a boat!) I have kept dozens of these small drawings Catherine drew, all with the happy sun. This is a part of our family history."

Catherine, *14" diameter, wool on linen. Adapted from the artwork of Catherine Mulcahy (at age three) and hooked by Beverley Mulcahy, Paxton, Massachusetts, 1996.*

"I found this drawing in a small sketchbook of mine that Catherine helped herself to. It is a self-portrait with a delightfully happy expression."

Children's Art | 71

Henry's Funny Man, *22" x 30", as-is wool on linen. Adapted from the artwork of Henry Joseph Jarrett (at age two) and hooked by Donna Reynolds, Princeton, Massachusetts, 2017.*

"Henry loved to draw a 'funny man' with his grandpa at the kitchen island. This is an enlargement of one funny man wearing a sweater and undies, slipping on the snow and ice. The rug was made in celebration of Henry's third birthday."

Inspirations for Children's Art

- Use a child's drawings to make coasters or mug rugs for the parents or grandparents.

- Use multiple drawings to create a sampler rug of the work of one child, or the art work of all the children in a family.

- Include children's names in the design, using their actual printing or script as a template.

- Print a label with the child's picture on it to show how they looked at the age they made the artwork. Include their age and any pertinent information about the piece.

Copyright Thoughts

Any piece of artwork is automatically copyright protected for the life of the artist plus 70 years. This protection includes art created by children. Ask their permission to use a child's artwork. Engage them in the process by telling them why you think it is a great piece and how it would look as a hooked rug. Try to stick with the colors that they used in the original as closely as possible.

If it is a black-and-white drawing, let the child help you decide on colors. Discuss size options, explaining that the drawing may have to be enlarged so that it is big enough to be hooked. Children are very honest and will tell you what they think. When I was adapting my daughter's artwork for *Noel, Noel*, she requested that I not make it into a pattern for other people to hook.

Chapter 8
It's All in a Name

HARVEY

Jack's Rug, 32" x 22", wool on linen. Designed and hooked by Norma Batastini, Glen Ridge, New Jersey, 2018.

Choosing a name for a baby is a big, important job for new parents. We consult books with lists of names and their meanings. Helpful relatives have suggestions. Family traditions pass down names from one generation to the next. There are the latest trends to consider. Whatever name is chosen, it lasts for a lifetime and becomes an important part of a person's identity.

Sometimes children get a nickname from a loving parent or a sibling, and that nickname sticks. Often as teenagers, children will want to use their full name or a different version of their name. My sister Elizabeth Jane has many names: Toot, Aunt Toot, Liz, Aunt Liz, and Betty Jane. It can be confusing to outsiders, but everyone in the family knows these names. What name would I use on a rug for her? Maybe for fun I'd use all of them. Think carefully about the name you choose to hook into a rug. You want the rug to last a lifetime.

The size of the rug is an important consideration. Will the rug be used in a certain area that requires specific dimensions? Will the rug be hung on the wall? What age is the child and what would they like? Would a pillow, tile, or wall hanging be more useful in a small room? With *Jack's Rug* and *Addison's Rug*, I kept the designs small. The 32" x 22" size can be used just inside or outside the doorway to announce whose room it is. Because that size is not intrusive, it could be hung on the wall at a later date or even taken off to a college dorm. It could also go to a first apartment where there may not be room for a large rug.

How will you design this name rug? Unless it is a surprise or the child is very young, ask the child what type of rug they would like. Getting their input will involve them in the process. An older child may want to have input on the motifs they would like to see, or may be willing to make some drawings that could be incorporated into the design.

You will have to decide how big the lettering will be and how much space to leave for other motifs. The location of the name on the rug is important. Generally, the name is placed in the center, but there are other artistic possibilities. In *Harvey* (page 77), the name is placed at the bottom, grounding the scene of New York harbor. In *Grace's Rug* (page 76) the name is located in the border. In *Samuel's Rug* (page 78), the name is curved in the center, reflecting the circular design of the rug.

When you are spacing letters on you pattern, be sure to leave plenty of room between each letter for possible outlining and for background.

There are many styles of lettering available, with myriad fonts and typefaces to choose from on every computer. Do you want simple block letters or something with more of a flourish?

Addison's Rug, 32" x 22", wool on linen. Designed and hooked by Norma Batastini, Glen Ridge, New Jersey, 2018.

Patterns provided on pages 118-119

Do you want printed or cursive letters? Printed letters are easier to hook. Cursive letters will give a flow to the name. Letters can be uppercase (capital) or lowercase. The name can be all capital letters, or the first letter can be a capital with the rest of the name in lowercase. A younger child's own blocky writing could be used; an older child might like their own signature.

For *Jack's Rug* and *Addison's Rug*, I used my own handwriting. That is how I write their names on gift tags and greeting cards. Over the years they will recognize their name as Grandma wrote it. On paper I played around with cursive and printed letters, with uppercase and lowercase letters. I wrote the samples in the size I would normally write so as not to distort the letters. After I got one that I was pleased with, I enlarged it to fit the size I allocated for the lettering.

Hooking letters can be a challenge but with a little care the lettering can be successful.

Choosing the type of wool is important. Use tightly woven wool that, when hooked, will form nice loops that stand up and hold their shape. Hook the loops slightly closer together than your usual hooking. There should be no gaps or spaces between the loops. After each letter is hooked, outline it with another color or fill in with background. This will help to keep the shape of the letter intact. Hook all of the loops to the same height and even with the background. Some people advocate hooking the letters higher. I prefer to keep them even unless I am hooking for a special effect.

If the name is the focal point of the rug, use colors that will stand out from the rest of the rug. Outlining the letters can make them more prominent. In *Henry* (page 81), each letter was hooked with a different color. In *Jack's Rug* (page 77), the large central letters were hooked with two bold colors, orange and navy blue. They show up well against the gray background. The first row of gray next to the navy blue is the lightest value of gray used. It becomes a highlight and makes the lettering more prominent. The outside border repeats those two colors, with three rows of navy blue. The edge is whipped with light gray yarn.

In *Addison's Rug*, the hot-pink letters consist of several wools blended together, including a tightly woven textured wool. Each letter has two rows of hooking for a bold effect—the letters show up well against the butter-colored background. Two rows of hot-pink wool were hooked along the outside edge. The finishing was done with two different color yarns: green yarn at the corners and pink yarn along the sides.

Grace's Rug, 25" x 22", dyed wool on monk's cloth. Designed and hooked by Lea McCrone, Malvern, Pennsylvania, 2012.

"After a succession of three sons and then three grandsons, I knew that granddaughter Grace would have to have a rug with lots of pink and purple in it. My son's love of elephants, and their living in Brooklyn, inspired this design. The mom, dad, and baby elephants are in front of a walkway to the Brooklyn Botanical Gardens, with the roses in bloom. The clover in the border is a nod to my daughter-in-law's Irish heritage."

Harvey, 38" x 27", *dyed wool on monk's cloth. Designed and hooked by Lea McCrone, Malvern, Pennsylvania, 2006.*

"My first grandson was born in New York City and for a short time lived in Battery Park, with an ever-changing panoramic view of the Hudson River. It was a page right out of a Richard Scarry book and became the inspiration for this rug. The figure and footprint in the lower right corner are sculptures by Tom Otterness, whose work is found throughout New York. The binocular lady is taking in the view, and the footprint leads through the children's play area. My son, Nathanael, and his wife, Anne, are at the railing. The 1931 John J. Harvey fireboat is now at Pier 66."

Artist's Statement: Lea McCrone

My artistic grandmother hooked rugs in the 1970s and, following in her footsteps, I started hooking about 30 years ago, using her old Rigby cutter and Puritan frame. At first, I worked on commercial patterns in fine cuts, then I hooked several of Beverly Conway's designs in #6 and #7 cuts. Soon, however, I began to create my own designs, usually with a specific recipient in mind. I find I am more invested in the process when working on my own idea. It's challenging, for sure, but more gratifying in the end.

Ideas begin with asking myself questions such as: Who are they? What do they love? Is there a story to tell, an occasion to celebrate? Do certain colors come to mind? All this goes through my mind as I sketch on paper.

Often photographs or other resources help me define my intentions.

My husband, Jerry, is great for getting perspectives right or for weeding out unnecessary elements. My designs have told the stories of my sister's barnyard animals, a son's graduation, an uncle's 1945 MG, my in-laws' Lake Erie cottage, and a friend's eighteenth-century family cottage in the Lake District in England. I even incorporated a trip to Prague into an ottoman. Last year, during our trip to Italy, I took many pictures of wonderful tiled floors, towns, and vineyards—there's probably a rug in there somewhere.

I use either monk's cloth or linen as backing, and my happy-place cut is a #6 or #7. I gravitate towards brighter colors, trying to establish contrast and to avoid the muddy middle zones, which are so easy for me to fall into. Now retired from a nursing career, I have more time to hook.

Samuel's Rug, 33" x 33", *dyed wool on monk's cloth. Designed and hooked by Lea McCrone, Malvern, Pennsylvania, 2009.*

"My daughter-in-law spends time in the Adirondacks with friends, and my family has New Hampshire as a summer destination. Sam has always loved animals, so I used wildlife from both of these regions in his rug. The purple moose and bear made the rug playful and fun to hook. As in my other rugs for grandchildren, there are special elements for him to identify."

Inspirations for Name Rugs

- Consider a variety of hooked items, not just rugs. Pillows, mug rugs, and signs make for fun gifts and are easy to display and store.

- Consider a rug with multiple names, maybe each child in a family.

- Use some of the child's drawings as motifs for the design.

- Add additional words that have meaning, such as the meaning of the name or a favorite saying.

- Use a nickname.

The Air Show, 36" x 24", hand-dyed wool on linen. Designed by Norma Batastini and hooked by Christine Dube, Williamsburg, Virginia, 2013.

"I hooked this rug for my grandson, Zachary. My husband, Tim, who flew remote-controlled biplanes when he was young, suggested the biplane design. The oval shape of the rug allows for the arrangement of the planes flying around the outer edge. The inner area was a perfect location for the name. I chose cheerful, bright colors. The rug is mounted on a wooden frame and hangs on the wall of Zachary's room."

Gus, 23" x 17", *wool on monk's cloth. Designed and hooked by Karen Bellinger, Fair Lawn, New Jersey, 2013. Karen used lots of leftover strips to hook this rug. She made a small rug that Gus would enjoy for years to come.*

Andrew, 23" x 17", *wool on monk's cloth. Designed and hooked by Karen Bellinger, Fair Lawn, New Jersey, 2013.*

Henry, 47" x 25", dyed wool on monk's cloth. Designed and booked by Lea McCrone, Malvern, Pennsylvania, 2007.

"I had fun with the letters in his name, using images he would recognize at the age of two or so, when I gave him his rug. I used a bright color palette and repeated colors throughout the piece. The subway tile background was a friend's idea."

Chapter 9

All Creatures Great and Small

Animals capture our imagination, and the vast animal kingdom provides endless inspiration for hooked rugs. Mammals, birds, fish, insects, reptiles, and amphibians inhabit our world. From early childhood, we are constantly exposed to these creatures. Farm animals are sources of food and clothing (think sheep) and are often the first animals a child is introduced to. Trips to zoos or wildlife refuges introduce a child to wild animals. As a young girl, I loved paging through an encyclopedia of animals, learning about their habits and habitats, picking my favorites. Grade-school children are often enthralled with dinosaurs. As they become teenagers, children become more aware of the relationship between humans and animals, some becoming activists working to protect animals; others becoming vegetarian because of new principles or beliefs.

Choose your project based on the child's interests. Young children prefer non-aggressive, soft and fuzzy creatures. A middle-school-age child may be taken with beetles and butterflies or may have developed an interest in bird-watching. Teens may be interested in exotics, like snakes, parrots, or iguanas. Everyone remembers the pets they had growing up, including cats, dogs, hamsters—and ponies, for the lucky!

Elephants . . . foxes . . . owls . . . penguins . . . giraffes. There are trends in the popularity of particular animals, likely based on the proliferation of animal-themed items from toy, clothing, and home decorating companies. Look to these sources to get ideas. After you have chosen an animal, decide on the style of the design. Will it be realistic, impressionistic, primitive, or cartoon-like?

For reference, collect pictures of the animal you have chosen. Use these visual references for body details and color placement. Visuals are especially useful for animals with overall patterns, such as zebras, giraffes, or tigers. Even if you are doing a cartoon-style animal, you will want to make sure the details—ears, eyes, and nose, for example—are correct.

Eyes are the most important feature of an animal's expression, emotion, and mood. Even primitive eyes need to be hooked with care. Count the number of loops used for the first iris and use the same number of loops for the other eye to keep them identical. Add an eye highlight to bring the animal to life.

Pattern provided on page 121

EDie Owl, 18"x 18", wool on linen. Designed by Norma Batastini and hooked by Elizabeth Deputy, Elverson, Pennsylvania, 2018.

"I hooked this whimsical owl in my favorite colors, pinks and purples. Keeping the design symmetrical was the most difficult part, as I didn't want uneven details to distract the eye. The perfect spot-dyed wool for the background was a creamy white with pinks and purples. I used the same wool to back the pillow."

Most animal shapes are unique, so they can be hooked in any color and still be identified. An elephant can be pink, an owl can be purple, and a moose can be blue. *EDie the Owl* was hooked in pink, purple, and lavender wool to fit a particular décor. The same colors were pulled out to the border. You can color plan your rug based on a room décor or a child's favorite color.

Use a variety of wools for hooking animals. Lots of textures will give the look of fur or fleece, making it easy to get a more realistic result.

A footstool is a wonderful gift for a child. *A Gathering of Teddy Bear Friends* exemplifies all the qualities needed for a successful piece. Each side of the stool has a different grouping of bears in delightful outfits. The blocks on the top, an iconic children's toy, add to the fun. The colors are soft and soothing but lively enough to keep the viewer's interest. The style of the stool would fit into any décor and not be outgrown. The hand-painted ball feet add a bit of whimsy. A sturdy footstool is also great for little ones learning to stand and walk because it cannot tip.

A Gathering of Teddy Bear Friends, 15" x 15", wool on linen. Designed and hooked by Loris Blandford, Frankford, Delaware, 2018.

Loris designed the footstool pattern to have four different series of teddy bears, one for each side of the stool. The best part of hooking the pattern was designing and color planning the bears' outfits. It is a great project that can be used in a nursery setting but will be cherished by children of all ages.

Maple, 30" x 30", wool on linen. Designed and hooked by Norma Batastini,
Glen Ridge, New Jersey, 2014.

How about hooking a rug for a pet? If you have a dog or a cat, you already know that they like to (or at least they try to!) cozy up to rug-hooking projects when these projects are left unattended. So many modern homes have hardwood floors, and a pet needs a soft place to lie down.

I designed *Maple* for my son's Goldendoodle, a gentle, sweet dog. Once when she was visiting, she chose one of my rugs to sleep on, so I decided that I would make a rug just for her. And I made her rug the same size as the rug she was first attracted to, 30" x 30". It was the perfect size! I used her silhouette as the main motif and hooked in a primitive style. I used many different types of wool, all in similar values, to hook Maple. (You can probably tell what color she is!) I hooked the background in organic hit-or-miss shapes in a variety of blue hues. I would only recommend hooking a rug for a pet if the pet is gentle and does not harm furniture or other furnishings.

Artist's Statement: Amy Tenzer

Hooking for me is an ongoing learning process. With every new piece I hook, I try a new stitch or a new embellishment. For *Dragonfly* I first looked at pictures of dragonflies to get ideas. Next came color planning.

As I planned, I figured out where and how to use the different kinds of fabrics I was given that I had never used before. How did they hook? How do I cut them? What do they look like next to each other, and how can I mix them with similarly dyed wool? I figured this out through trial and lots of errors, and with the helpful advice from other hookers—how to cut velour; why to tear, not cut, silk into big pieces for hooking. I learned that metallic and dichroic wool (see note) was very hard to cut and hook, and did not like being unhooked. For me, these worked best as small accent areas.

Norma suggested that the dragonfly needed to be outlined. I hesitated doing this until the background went in because I don't like outlining. But she was right, and I went back and outlined the wings and body mostly with embroidery thread—it was easier to squeeze in than even #3-cut wool. The embroidery thread added texture and a dimensional element to the dragonfly when I hooked it higher than the wool loops. When the dragonfly was still not standing out enough from the background, I added buttons to the wings.

The background was a challenge. I wanted to suggest movement, so straight directional hooking was out. Wavy lines across the canvas worked for a while but it was not giving me the effect I wanted. I like to try new stitches and have wanted to try "pebbling" or random fill. I used it in a couple of spaces between the wavy lines—and it worked. It added a textural element to the background.

Finally, knowing when to stop was a challenge. There was always another shade of purple, or some additional buttons, or a couple of loops of exotic wool I wanted to add to see if they made the dragonfly more exciting. I found how to end this hooking adventure with some specialty yarn I have been saving. It was the perfect finishing touch for the dragonfly, making a border that echoed all of the colors in the piece.

Note: Dichroic wool has an overlay material applied to it that gives a holographic effect similar to dichroic glass. This type of wool was developed by Ania Knap to use in a rug featuring a peacock.

Pattern provided on page 117

Dragonfly, 14½" x 16", hand-dyed wool, dichroic and metallic wool, velour, hand-dyed silk, sari silk, embroidery thread, beads, and buttons on linen. Designed by Norma Batastini and hooked by Amy Tenzer, Short Hills, New Jersey, 2018.

"The Dragonfly *pattern came with many unusual and brightly colored wools, silks, and velvety soft velour. I couldn't resist trying everything out and I created a dragonfly that a child would love. It was an adventure using all the unusual fibers and trying creative stitches. The challenge was not letting the dragonfly get overwhelmed by the background. This was solved, in part, by adding some embellishments and hooking higgledy-piggledy in the background."*

Inspirations for Animal Rugs

- Design a rug with all of the animals that start with the same letter, animals of the same color, or different animals of the same species.

- Use animals, birds, and insects in your neighborhood.

- Design a rug with all of the animals seen on a special trip. The child could keep a list as your travel.

- Hook the child's pets. Cats and dogs are favorites, but don't forget hamsters, iguanas, or parrots.

- Make a rug the shape of an animal. A rounded shape like a whale, pig, or hippo is easiest to finish.

Copyright Thoughts

Animal shapes and colors are not protected by copyright. Draw your own animals using reference materials and field guides to check for details and sizing. Or have the child draw the animal for you.

Some of the following items are protected:

- Disney copyrights its animated characters such as Simba; generic lions are not protected. All animated movies and cartoons are protected.

- Cartoon animals such as Snoopy, Garfield, and Bugs Bunny are protected.

- Stuffed animals in a specific style, like the Care Bears, are protected—but not the generic teddy bear.

- Magical creations or fantasy creatures created by a company or individual artist are protected. Examples would be Shrek or Smurfs.

Whimsical Cat, 12" x 12", #3-cut wool on linen. Adapted from the artwork of Denis Gordon and hooked by Diane Cellar, Madison, New Jersey, 2018.

This small cat design is adapted from an oil painting purchased in Boothbay Harbor, Maine, in 2012. It was challenging to locate the artist to ask for copyright permission. After talking with the gallery that displayed Gordon's work, Diane located the artist in Albuquerque, New Mexico, in 2017. The artist was flattered that Diane wanted to replicate the painting in wool and granted permission to use the cat in a hooked piece and publish the image.

Grasshopper, *34" x 26", wool on linen. Designed by Off the Hook Wool Rugs
and hooked by Joan Thomas, Fair Haven, New Jersey, 2017.*

*"I wanted a colorful rug and a subject—a bug—that would appeal to my youngest grandson, Nicolas. My teacher,
Michele Micarelli, challenged my color comfort zone, which made this rug a lot of fun to hook."*

Jungle Animals, 26" x 26", wool on monk's cloth. Designed by Norma Batastini and hooked by Mary Anne Buonadies, Wyckoff, New Jersey, 2018.

"I wanted a rug with jungle animals for my grandson, Landon. He loves animals and admired a rug I hooked for my son Matt in 1994. We added the toy monkey so it would be like his Uncle Matt's rug."

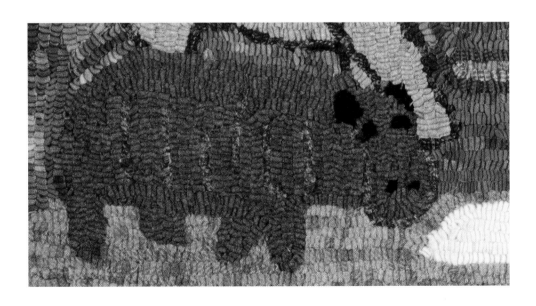

Peaceable Kingdom, *40" x 36", wool on monk's cloth. Designed by Patsy Becker and hooked by Mary Anne Buonadies, Wyckoff, New Jersey, 1995.*

"My son saw a Peaceable Kingdom *painting, by Edward Hicks, in Cooperstown, New York. I hooked this version but removed the flamingo and added his favorite toy monkey."*

Sock Monkey, *23" x 34", #6-cut wool on monk's cloth. Designed by Beverly Conway and hooked by Ellen Savage, Pottstown, Pennsylvania, 2012.*

"The colors were selected to match sock monkey dolls often made by grandmothers (including me—I made some for my grandkids). It is not a difficult rug to hook. I keep it at my house and enjoy imagining how my grandchildren will react to it when they visit."

Pattern provided on page 120

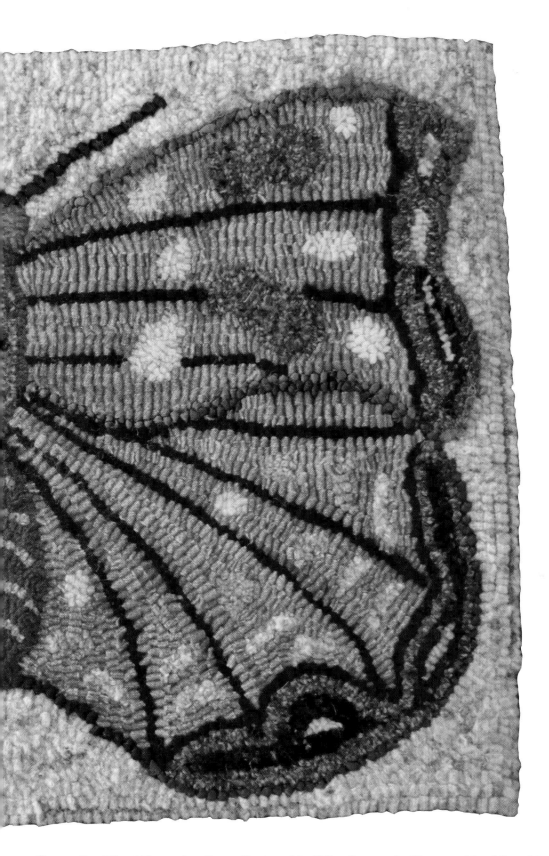

Butterfly, *17" x 12", wool on linen. Designed by Ellen Savage for Heart in Hand Rug Hooking and hooked by Lydia Brenner, Fair Haven, New Jersey, 2018.*

"After researching various butterflies, I hooked this butterfly using my favorite colors instead of realistic ones. I'd be thrilled to see a butterfly with these colors. My infant granddaughter will be, too, and this butterfly will land in her room."

Graduation Days

There are many milestones throughout a child's young life. As parents, friends, and family members, we feel the emotional significance of these changes. Stepping over these thresholds changes the life of everyone involved—sadness that a childhood is over and joy for what is to come next.

The biggest change for my family was high school graduations. Now it was time for my children to follow their dreams and pursue the studies and activities that were most important to them. Graduations are new beginnings—leaving home for college, military service, or a new job: the first steps to adulthood.

As rug hookers, we celebrate these moments with specially designed rugs. The examples shown in this chapter are all college graduation rugs. All were designed for a specific child—sometimes with input and sometimes not.

Before you begin to design a graduation rug, first consider the size you want the finished rug to be. Will it be a rug? A wall hanging? A pillow? That will guide your design choices.

Many college campuses have beautiful old buildings that exemplify the spirit of the campus. To capture the feel of a building, first determine the primary architectural details that define it. The amount of detail you can include will be decided by the cut of wool you want to use and the overall size of the design. For instance, a small rug in a wide cut of wool would be able to show only the basic elements of a building; a large rug in a fine cut of wool would be able to show the basic elements and many of the smaller details.

Middlebury, 20" x 24", wool on linen. Designed by Norma Batastini and hooked by Jane Whitley, Mahwah, New Jersey, 2009.

Jane's grandson graduated from Middlebury College in Vermont. His main college sport was football so it was important to show the fieldhouse. The panther is the school mascot, and the chapel is a prominent building on the campus.

The two Lehigh University rugs are fine examples of hooking a pictorial rug. *Kyle's Graduation Rug* is a winter scene, using muted colors with a blue-gray sky. Gail Ferdinando used a variety of green wools to show the flowing lawn and to define different areas, like the Adirondack seating. She hooked the students simply and scattered them throughout the lawn, giving a sense of activity on campus. This is a small rug with a large building, so Gail used #3- and #4-cut wools for the hooking.

Eric's Lehigh Graduation is larger, so Debbie Walsh used a variety of cuts of wool (#3 to #8). In Debbie's rug, the scene is autumn, with brightly colored leaves and a bright turquoise sky. She used many types of green wools, with the darkest value showing shadows cast by the trees. The colors in the front of the lawn are brighter, working back to softer and duller colors along the horizon.

Both Debbie and Gail used artistic license when designing their rugs, including certain details and eliminating others, all dependent on the story they wanted to tell.

Many college students participate in sports, whether on their school teams or on intramural teams. They can be represented by team logos, mascots, and colors. In Middlebury, Jane Whitley portrayed the fieldhouse to show her grandson's participation on the football team. Consider music and drama activities, especially if your students perform in different roles on stage. Classroom work and majors can also be included—after all, these are the main reason for going to college! Clubs, sororities, and fraternities are important to some students. Many friendships made at college last a lifetime, so consider making friends part of the rug design. Let your imagination lead you to your design.

Eric's Lehigh Graduation, 53" x 42", wool on linen. Designed and hooked by Debbie Walsh, Pittstown, New Jersey, 2015.

"I hooked this rug for my son Eric to celebrate his graduation from Lehigh University. I wanted to portray a sense of the beautiful campus and worked from several photographs I took. The most difficult part was how to include the path that welcomes you to campus. The border, inspired by the stained-glass ceiling in the library, is one of my favorite parts of the rug. Jen Lavoie helped me with some of the design elements and the hooking of the rug."

Artist's Statement: Gail Ferdinando

When my son, Kyle, was a junior in college, I wanted to hook him a rug commemorating his college years. He loved the idea and I was happy that he wanted to be involved in the design process. We talked about the things that meant the most to him during his four years at Lehigh University. He spent a lot of time on the grassy area in front of the beautiful Old Main campus building, and since it also had the university name and graduation year in mulch out front, we made it the central part of the rug. He also spent a lot of time in the library, another old and beautiful building on campus, so we included that as well. And lastly, his fraternity was depicted in the rug.

After making line drawings of all the buildings (by tracing them from photos) we played with the design by moving the buildings around.

After placing the main campus building in the center, we put the library to the left to balance the tall right side of the main building. The fraternity house did not seem to fit in anywhere (plus the fact that it was not such a nice-looking building!), so we instead included the rock with the Greek fraternity letters which sits outside the fraternity house. The Adirondack chairs, the students walking around campus, and the flagpole and walkways were all added last to give a feel of being on campus. And a simple dark border holds it all in. It was done in time for Kyle's graduation (phew!) and he was as thrilled as I was with the finished rug.

Kyle's Graduation 2014, 32" x 24", *dyed and as–is wool on linen. Designed by Kyle Ferdinando and Gail Ferdinando, and hooked by Gail Ferdinando, Pittstown, New Jersey, 2014.*

Inspirations for Graduation Rugs

- Hook the student and their friends with the clothes and styles that are currently popular. It will become a part of their history.

- Add a border with names of friends, classes taken, or activities they participated in.

- Make a smaller project with the school colors and logo as pillow, tiles, or signs.

- Create a story rug, showing the progression from kindergarten to graduation.

- Isolate a special moment and honor it in your design.

Copyright Thoughts

A school logo is protected under trademark law. A logo may also include original artwork that is protected by copyright. In 1992, the US Court of Appeals for the Ninth Circuit considered a case concerning this topic, producing "The Nominative Use Doctrine." It states that a person may use a trademark without permission as a reference to another product or entity. In these cases, the least amount of the logo should be used and the user should not suggest that he or she is affiliated with the product in any way.

For example, Andy Warhol used the Campbell's soup label in his iconic artwork. Campbell could probably have stopped him from publishing and displaying his artwork. A company has the prerogative to decide if the artwork is detrimental to its brand. The artwork may infringe upon copyright law but it may also promote their brand in other ways, like free advertising.

If the logo is distorted in an artistic way and this version can be confused with the original, it may be in violation of the law. A company could be offended by the artwork and not want their brand presented that way. School logos can be used in your artwork without permission if you follow the guidelines of the "Nominative Use Doctrine." Always present the logo as originally conceived and not to the detriment of the school.

Elon University, *20" x 24", wool on linen. Designed by Norma Batastini and hooked by
Jane Whitley, Mahwah, New Jersey, 2011.*

*Jane's granddaughter graduated from Elon in 2011. Included in the design are her initials, her graduation
year, and her sorority. The building is the main campus office building and typical of the architecture of this
southern school.*

Elise's Graduation Rug, *19" x 25", wool strips, yarn, and embroidery thread on linen. Designed by Lydia Brenner and Norma Batastini, and hooked by Lydia Brenner, Fair Haven, New Jersey, 2013.*

"I hooked this rug for my daughter Elise to celebrate her graduation from the University of Virginia. I took photos of places important to her and representative of the grounds. I added dogwood blossoms to the upper corners to pull the design together. The lower right corner of the rug represents Beta Bridge, which is painted with messages almost daily by the students. My message to my daughter: Congratulations!"

CONGRATS ELISE '13!

OWA! LD

Final Thoughts

> "One of the greatest dignities of humankind is that each successive generation is invested in the welfare of each new generation." —Fred Rogers

Involve Family in the Process

Families, and especially children, are the most important parts of our life. No wonder the whole process of hooking rugs for the children in our lives brings us such pleasure and joy! Now that you have read about all the kinds of rug-hooking projects that you can make for children of all ages, I hope that you will be inspired to plan a hooked piece for that special child in your life. Perhaps you have been introduced to projects that you had never even thought of.

Every step of imagining, designing, choosing colors and wools, and hooking your rug is a step that, ultimately, will give you pleasure and satisfaction. The love with which you brought your project to completion will show through in your work.

And you will be sharing your art with the next generation. Whatever project you make will be appreciated now and for many years to come. Talk with your family when planning a new project for a child so that their ideas can be considered and incorporated. Usually opinions will abound! If the piece is to be a surprise, be sure of your choices—especially those of color, subject, and size.

Involve the family with the project and you will get some ideas that you may not have come up with on your own. Everyone has a different perspective; great ideas can come from conversation and discussion. You may have some basic ideas that are enhanced by seeing them through someone else's eyes. It's like taking a basic recipe and improving upon it. Leave open spaces in the design; if other ideas come up during the hooking, you will have room to add them.

Making a rug involves a lot of quiet work, and each loop represents the passage of time. The brain is usually busy as new ideas for color, techniques, or design will pop into your head. Listen for these ideas—the additions may make the rug a masterpiece.

Adding a Label

Making your own label will allow you to include as much information as you want. I usually type up the information on my computer and then print the information onto pre-cut muslin sheets. You can also write the information directly onto muslin using a pen that is permanent on fabric. Add small drawings or decorative shapes along the borders. Sign your name as the child knows it; over a lifetime of signing cards and gift tags, your signature will be recognized and cherished.

Another option is to have all of the information embroidered on rug tape before applying to the back of the rug. For pillows, you might appliqué or embroider your name or initials on the back.

Three-dimensional pieces are more challenging to label. In those cases, add your name or initials into the actual hooking. If all the information you want to include is extensive and would be too big for a label, you can write or print out the information, then place the folded paper in a special pocket sewn onto the piece.

When you rug is finished, document it. Adding identifying information will increase its importance as a part of your family history and will also increase the rug's monetary value. Include the obvious information: your name, the designer, and the date. Add other information that adds meaning to the gift.

You may even come up with an idea for a special personal touch. Turn the page for examples. The label for *Dragonfly*, by Amy Tenzer, is simply written on a piece of grosgrain ribbon and embellished with a dragonfly charm. Sandy Francisco included Mom-Mom, the name her grandson calls her, on *I Think I Can.* A label with a bee skep design contains all of the information on Debi Roeder's rug, *Grace's Farm*, including the name of her granddaughter who drew the picture.

Be sure to give instructions about use and caring for the piece. I always encourage the recipient to use the hooked piece. If something happens to it, it is not a disaster—anything can be fixed. Pulled loops, small stains, and worn binding can be replaced. I also give general care instructions: light vacuuming or washing with mild suds. Wool is very resilient and will wear and age well. If you have used alternative materials, you may have to give more detailed care instruction.

Once the rug is given as a gift, let go! The recipient will decide how and when they want to use the rug.

*Label for **Dragonfly**, by Amy Tenzer (page 86)*

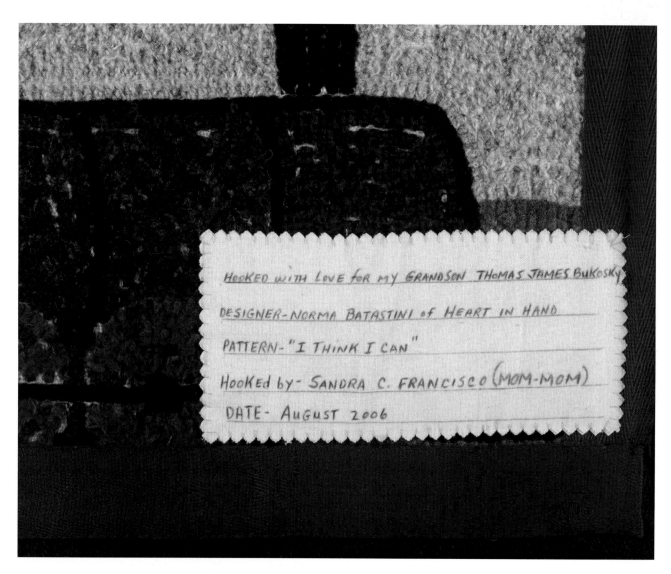

*Label for **I Think I Can**, by Sandy Francisco (page 58)*

*Label for **Grace's Farm**, by Debi Roeder (page 68)*

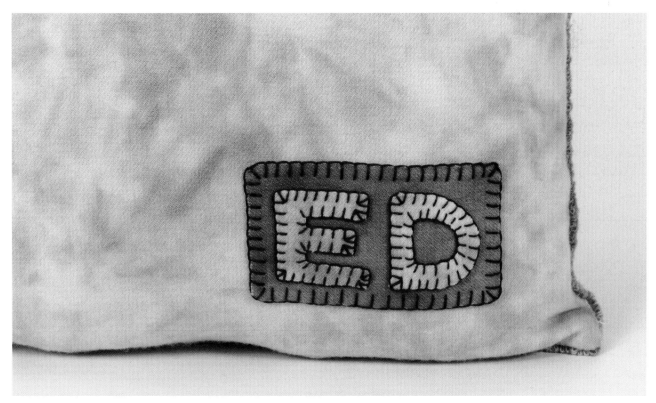

*Label for **EDie**, by Elizabeth Deputy (page 83)*

Project Patterns

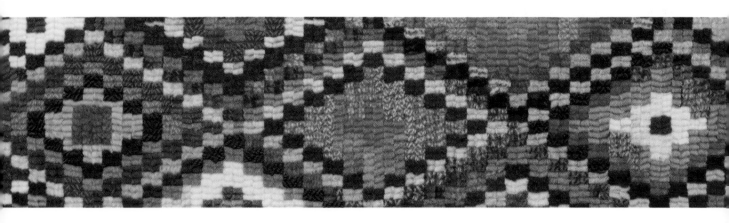

A Pattern for You:

Baby Blocks

Baby blocks have been a popular children's toy for ages. Antique-style blocks or contemporary blocks spelling our specific messages are also used decoratively in many settings. The samples in these four block designs have 4" faces; after constructed with hooking and batting, they measure 5" on all sides, but you can enlarge to any size you like. To soften the look, I hooked them with a neutral background. I used gray plaid to outline each area so it would match up easily when sewn together. These blocks hooked in very bright colors would also be attractive to children.

I like the 4" size because they are easy for young children to pick up when small-motor skills have not developed. They are also lightweight and would not be a hazard if tossed. The blocks can offer lots of play opportunities, such as identifying the motifs and colors. Be sure to sing "The Alphabet Song" too!

To assemble the blocks:

1. Hook and steam the pieces.

2. Use a zigzag stitch to sew as close as possible to the hooked edge to prevent raveling.

3. Cut away the excess backing and reinforce the inside corners.

4. Use a ladder stitch to sew the blocks together, leaving one side open to insert foam. (Heavy-duty thread is best.)

5. Purchase pieces of foam cut to the size of your blocks.

6. Wrap the foam blocks with fabric or batting as needed to fit the shape of the constructed block.

7. Place wrapped foam block inside and sew up the last seams, again using the ladder stitch.

As seen on page 5.

Baby Blocks

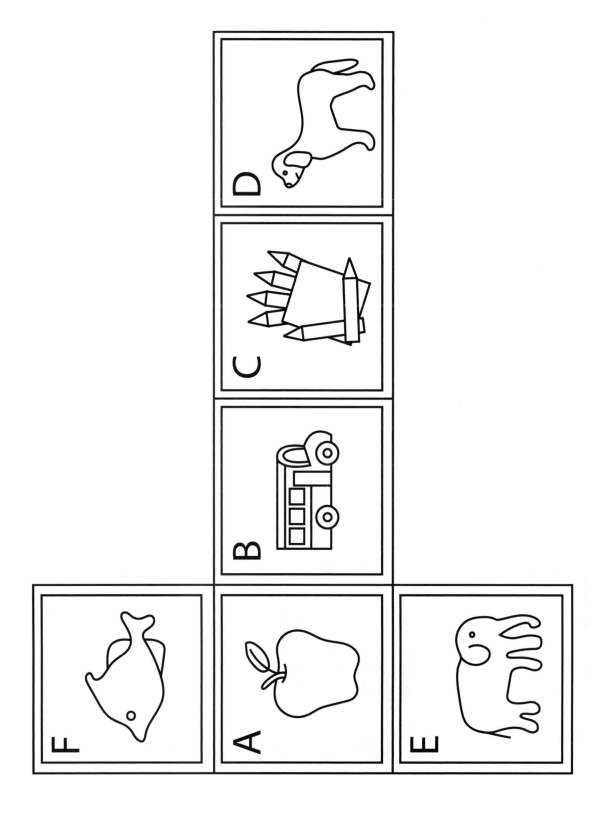

Baby Blocks

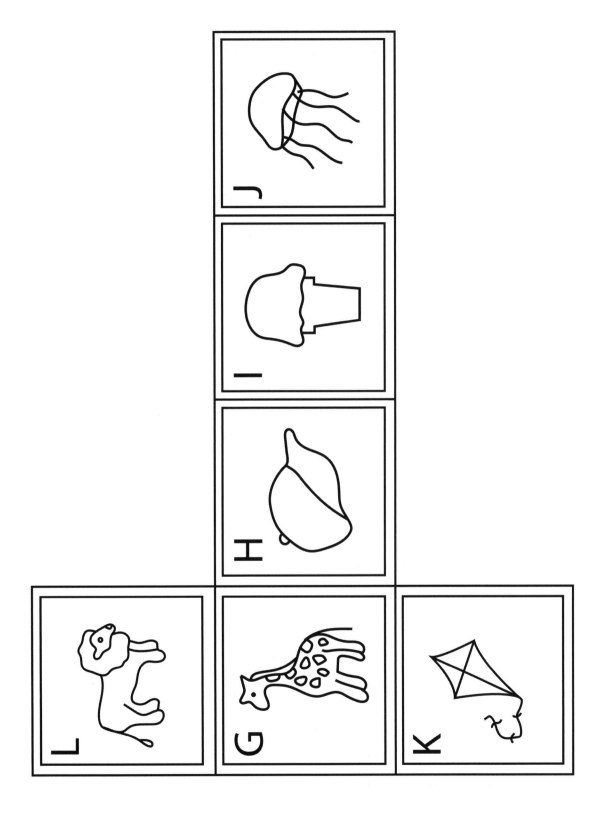

Baby Blocks

Baby Blocks

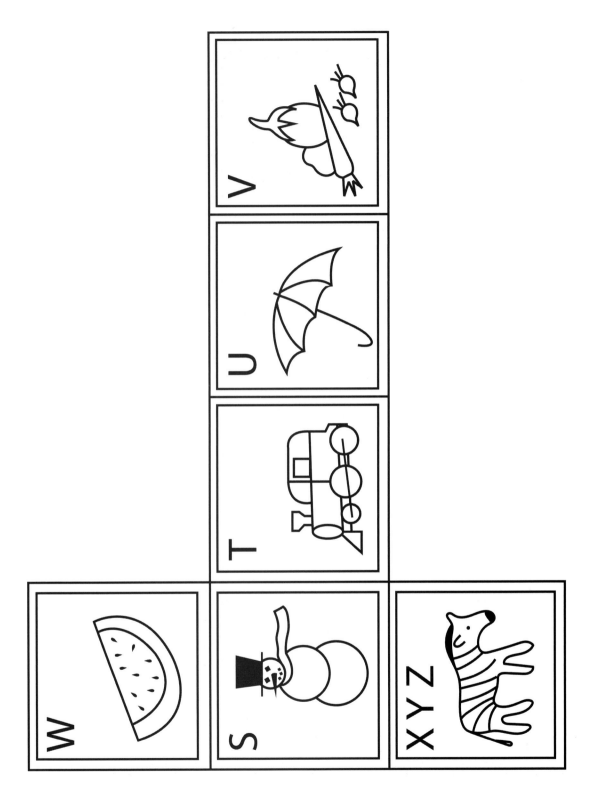

A Pattern for You:

I'm a Little Teapot

You may enlarge the pattern to any size. The sample size is 21" x 20". Personalize the pattern by adding a border with all of the words in the rhyme. The teapot design can be changed to match a favorite teapot in your home.

As seen on page 18.

A Pattern for You:

Trust Me

I designed this rug based on the story of Daniel in the Lions' Den for Cyndi Stinson. As a retired teacher and a minister's wife, a biblical story had lots of appeal. To prepare, I read the Bible story again to get the details right. Then I researched paintings of the Great Masters to see how they had portrayed the story. After studying the paintings of Peter Paul Rubens, Briton Rivière, Robert Ambrose Dudley, and Jean-Baptiste Auguste Leloir, I noted several important elements: The lions were to be front and center—and lots of them. They are fun to hook and add drama to the scene. And the sky or light from above needed to be seen. The color of the sky would relieve the dense colors of the den and also symbolize hope.

As seen on page 30.

A Pattern for You:

Puppet

This generic puppet pattern is a jumping-off place for you to design your own puppet based on the story you would like to tell. Enlarge to the size you need, but remember you want it to fit comfortably on your hand or a child's hand.

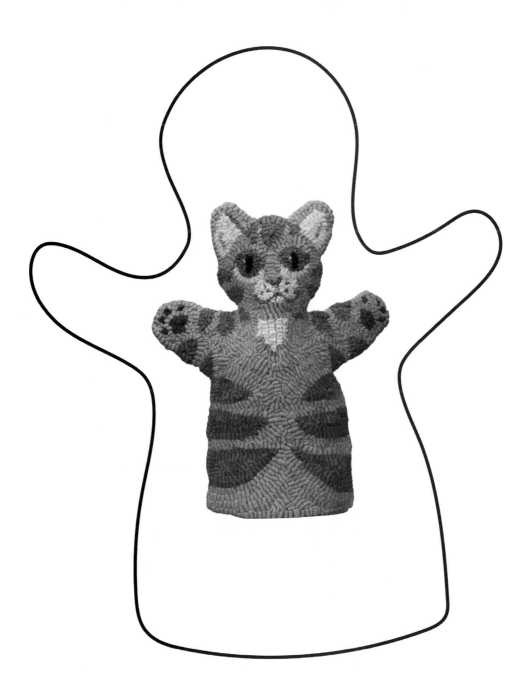

As seen on page 40.

A Pattern for You:

Tic-Tac-Toe

Tic-tac-toe is a classic game played with pencil and paper. Younger children will enjoy this hooked version, especially as they are still developing fine-motor skills needed for writing. The size of this rug makes it usable on the floor or a table. Little hands can easily pick up the playing pieces. Sandy Francisco conveniently has four grandchildren, so their names fit on the border, one on each side. If you have more names, they can be spaced evenly all around the border.

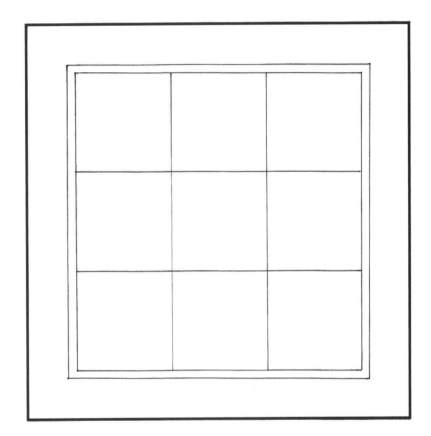

As seen on page 48.

A Pattern for You:

I Think I Can

When I was growing up, the story "The Little Engine That Could," by Watty Piper, was a favorite. It has suspense, action, and great life lessons of hard work and optimism. Trains are very popular toys, and today there are many train characters in books, movies, and television shows that have generated related—and copyrighted—merchandise. With this generic pattern you can personalize the train to your tastes. Choose colors to coordinate with the child's room, add a border with words, or change the landscape to a favorite locale. Enlarge this to whatever size you prefer. For a rug 40" x 12", enlarge it by 600%.

As seen on page 58.

A Pattern for You:

Dragonfly

The original size of this mat is 14½" x 16". For a finished design of approximately that size, enlarge this pattern 325%. For sparkles and interest, enhance with special fabrics, beads, and the like.

As seen on page 86.

A Pattern for You:

Floral Border and Geometric Border

The original size of these rugs is 32" x 22". You may enlarge to any size suitable for you. Add the child's name to the center section. *Addison's Rug* is more feminine, with a flower border. The hit-or-miss inner border allows for maximum use of color. *Jack's Rug* is more masculine, with a geometric design featuring both a hit-or-miss outer border and an inner border of circles hooked as hit-or-miss.

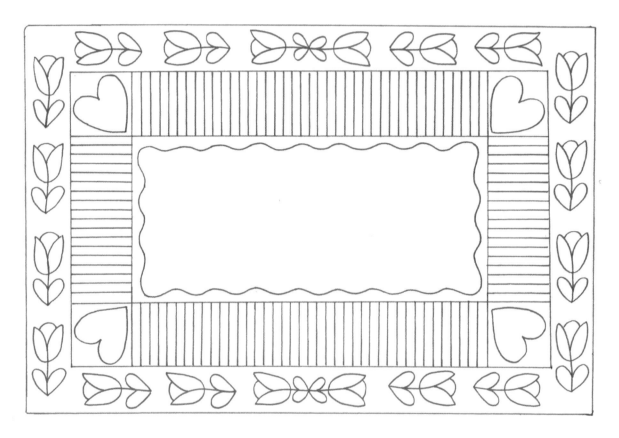

As seen on page 8.

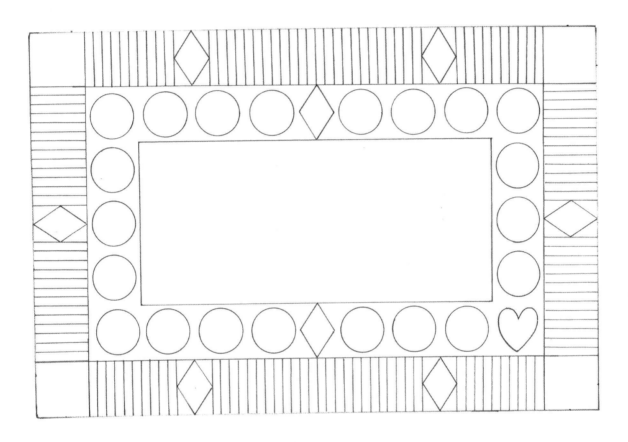

As seen on page 9.

A Pattern for You:

Butterfly

The original mat is 17" x 12". For a mat approximately that size, enlarge this design 300%. Make your loved one a realistic butterfly, or use your imagination!

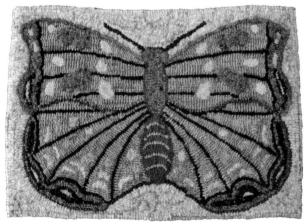

As seen on page 92.

A Pattern for You:

EDie Owl

Use this design as a pillow or rug. The original size is 18" x 18". Enlarge to your preferred size. The whimsical owl can be hooked in any color plan. In the hooked pillow shown here, the background is a spot-dyed wool hooked in an echo pattern around the owl, working out from the scalloped edge. To change up the pattern, add a branch for the owl to perch on.

As seen on page 83.

Resources

- Heart in Hand Rug Hooking, Glen Ridge, New Jersey, 973-746-2936, or G_Batastini@msn.com. Designs, wool and supplies by Norma Batastini.

- Wool and Goods, LLC, York, Maine, www.woolandgoods.com. Kathy Spellacy's shop features the patterns of Patsy Becker.

- Yankee Peddler, Killingworth, Connecticut, www.yankeepeddler.com.

- Prairie Craft House, by Carol Kassera, Aledo, Texas, ktimberman69@msn.com.

- Holly Hill Designs, by Susan Quicksall, Oglesby, Texas, www.hollyhilldesigns.net.

- The Wool Farm, Frankford, Delaware, www.facebook.com/TheWoolFarm. Patterns and supplies for stools, hand dyed wool, and alpaca.

- Polly Minick Designs, Naples, Florida. Available from A Nimble Thimble, www.animblethimble.com; Minickandsimpson.blogspot.com.

- Heavens to Betsy, Claverack, New York, www.heavens-to-betsy.com.

- Honey Bee Hive, Manchester, Connecticut, www.rughook.com.

- American Country Rugs, Pawlet, Vermont, www.americancountryrugs.com.

- Bev Conway Designs, Middlebury, Vermont.

- Off the Hook Wool Rugs, Walnut Creek, California, www.offthehookwoolrugs.com.

Your Free Trial Of
R·U·G
HOOKING
MAGAZINE

Join the premium community for rug hookers! Claim your FREE, no-risk issue of *Rug Hooking* Magazine.

Sign up to receive your free trial issue (a $9.95 value).

Love the magazine? Simply pay the invoice for one full year (4 more issues for a total of 5).

Don't love the magazine? No problem! Keep the free issue as our special gift to you, and you owe absolutely nothing!

Get a Free No-Risk Issue

Claim Your FREE Trial Issue Today!

Call us toll-free to subscribe at (877) 297 - 0965
Canadian customers call (866) 375 - 8626
Use PROMO Code: **RRTY18**

 -

Discover inspiration, techniques & patterns in every issue!

Yes! Rush my FREE issue of *Rug Hooking* Magazine and enter my subscription. If I love it, I'll simply pay the invoice for $34.95* USD for a one year subscription (4 more issues for a total of 5). If I'm not satisfied, I'll return the invoice marked "cancel" and owe absolutely nothing.

SEND NO MONEY NOW-WE'LL BILL YOU LATER

Cut out (or copy) this special coupon and mail to:
Rug Hooking Magazine Subscription Department
PO Box 2263, Williamsport, PA 17703-2263

First Name   Last Name

Postal Address   City   State/Province   Zip/Postal Code

Email Address

* Canadian subscribers add $5/year for S&H + taxes.
Please allow 6-8 weeks for delivery of the first issue.

RRTY18